IN THE ARENA

By

ISOBEL KUHN

MOODY PRESS

CHICAGO

FOREWORD

DEAR LORD JESUS,

I want to write a love letter to You. Not the ordinary I-love-you kind. Nor the usual just-between-you-and-me kind; for others will read what I write. Something like Elizabeth Barrett Browning's:

> How do I love Thee?
> Let me count the ways.

And yet not like that one either, for the subject of this letter is not to be my love for You. That has been too puny, too shoddy, too besmirched with failure to be a theme.

I want this letter to be a revelation of *You*. When people read it I want them to see *You*. When they find me in a perfectly hopeless situation, as so often I was, I want them to know clearly it was You who pulled me out. I want them to see Your infinite patience, Your unwavering faithfulness. Although You work so silently, so delicately, there is a "shining forth" when You are present. But how can one make others see it?

Lord, dear, please will You help me write it? I cannot put Your beauty into words, but if I can show You working in the background of all that happened (even as I watched You) that will be enough. As You did reveal Yourself to me, please reveal Yourself to them!

Your own—by right of purchase, then by self-surrender,

ISOBEL S. KUHN

3

CONTENTS

EXPLAINING OUR TITLE

1940: We were missionaries on the China-Burma border, and had just received word that, owing to new dangers from the Japanese war, our Mission was not allowing schoolchildren whose parents lived far away to go home for the holidays. This meant that our Kathryn, who was in the China Inland Mission school at Chefoo, would not be able to reach us. As it was more than a year since she had seen her parents, it was decided that I try to reach her. This meant travel on the Burma Road. And at one place it meant that I had to thumb a ride with a Chinese truck. I would, of course, pay for my passage, but this was the only way of procuring a vehicle at that time and place.

So that raw November day saw me standing in the middle of the road, holding up my thumb to a Chinese driver, who was careening merrily along toward me. I have always felt that womanly women did not do such things, and only desperate necessity would ever have made me willing. But a mother who wants to reach her child will go through much, so there I was, holding up my thumb to this Chinese young fellow, who drew his truck to a standstill and grinned at me. We bargained for a seat, and he doubtless never dreamed that this drab, middle-aged, white woman was cringing with humiliation inside. But I was. Reasonable or not, I have never forgotten that flush of shame.

Once quietly installed in the truck, I talked in my heart to Him who has always been my refuge. "Lord, why do I have to be put in such situations as this?" And immediately the words came: *For I think that God hath set forth us . . . last . . . for we are made a spectacle unto the world* (I Cor. 4:9).

A spectacle—that was just how I had felt. But it would never have been necessary, if I had not become a missionary to a primitive people in those back-of-beyond places. So it was, indirectly, for Christ's sake, and the thought comforted me.

As I had to spend many hours just seated in the truck as the trip continued, I had plenty of time to ponder. It might seem absurd to some to appropriate such a wonderful verse to oneself for such a paltry trial as a few minutes of humiliation. Obviously Paul was referring to the terrible Arena experiences of his day, when Christians were thrown to the wild beasts to make a Roman holiday. And yet, as Amy Wilson Carmichael points out, our Lord stoops to our small cries as well as to our great ones. "Mizar means littleness—from the little hill. The land of Jordan was a place where great floods (the swelling of the Jordan) might terrify the soul . . . but Mizar was only a little hill: and yet the word is *'I will remember Thee from . . . the hill Mizar. . . .'* The Lord will command His lovingkindness, even to us in our little hill."

I had cried unto Him from a very little Mizar and that verse had flashed back to me like an answer. "A spectacle—for Him." Was I willing?

Through the several years which followed, years of war strain and danger, this thought kept returning to me. The different trials of us Christians of the twentieth century are like so many platforms in the world's arena of today. The unbeliever looks on at our struggles and is only impressed or influenced if he sees the power of God working there. The purpose of the arena experience is not for our punishment; it is that God might be revealed.

George Matheson had an arena experience, and because of this impending calamity his fiancée broke their engagement. That alone would not make him a spectacle. But the comforting power of his God came down upon him at that dark hour, lifted him to spiritual vision, and caused him to write:

> O Love, that will not let me go,
> I rest my weary soul in Thee;
>
> . . . .
>
> O Light, that followest all my way,
> I yield my flickering torch to Thee;
>
> . . . .
>
> O Joy, that seekest me through pain,
> I cannot close my heart to Thee;
>
> . . . .
>
> O Cross, that liftest up my head,
> I dare not ask to fly from Thee;
> I lay in dust life's glory dead,
> And from the ground, there blossoms red,
> Life that shall endless be.

That spectacle of the brilliant, soon-to-be-sightless young man, forsaken by his earthly love, yet bathed and upheld in Christ's, has halted many a sinner on the way to Hell. George Matheson's blindness has revealed God to many another. It was not given to punish Matheson. It was allowed to manifest the power of God to bring blessing to the world.

So God taught me through the years to view my own trials as platforms in today's arena. I thought this concept was original with me, but one day my husband found that Hudson Taylor had formed the same opinion many years ago. He said: "Difficulties afford a platform upon which He can show Himself. Without them we could never know how tender, faithful, and almighty our God is." I found it so too.

From a bed of sickness I have had time to quietly review my life, and as I gazed it seemed that my most valuable lessons have been learned on these platforms. How often I have failed Him, I do not like to think. But of His tenderness and faithfulness there was never an end. As you read, I pray that you may not focus attention on how dark the trial, but rather on the power of God that was manifested there, and *the emergence into light*.

One of my dear editors asked why I did not begin at the beginning. How did I become a Christian? When was I impressed to be a missionary? Were not those experiences platforms too?

Perhaps they were. I groped my way out of agnosticism for about two years; those adventures are more book-length than chapter-length. Conversion and consecration were simultaneous with me, and so my first platform was when I suddenly became conscious of *the fight* in the arena. Groping toward Himself, secretly, privately, I suddenly found my life clashing with another life; I found I could not live to myself alone. Unexpectedly I was on a platform, spotlighted, grappling for that which had become more precious than life to me. I did not know it at the time, but I was in the arena—*for Christ*.

CHAPTER ONE

OBSTACLES

"IF YOU GO TO CHINA, it will be over my dead body. I will never consent," was my mother's bitter remark.

I sat with my mouth open, staring at her in aghast silence. My dear mother, who had first taught me to love the Lord Jesus, who had been president of the Women's Missionary Society in the Canadian Presbyterian church for as long as I could remember, who had opened her home to the China Inland Mission for prayer meetings. My dear mother, who was all that, to be so bitter because her daughter felt called of God to be a missionary?

"If you want to do Christian work, that is fine. You could be a YWCA secretary here in Canada. That is quite a respectable position. But a foreign missionary! Only those who cannot find work to do at home or who are disappointed in love go to the foreign field," Mother continued, bitter in her opposition.

Again my mouth fell open in utter amazement. Such an appraisal of a foreign missionary call had never entered my head before. Could it be true?

I had just returned from ten wonderful days at The Firs Conference in Bellingham, Washington. Foreign missionaries had been there, including Mr. J. O. Fraser, of the China Inland Mission, who had told us how he had opened the Lisu tribe of the China-Burma border to the Gospel. What had taken him to China? Lack of a job? Disappointment in love? At the moment I knew nothing of Mr. Fraser's brilliant career at London University, and I knew nothing of his private life. But I brushed both motives aside as absolutely incongruous. If I could know God as J. O. Fraser did—if my life could be as sweetly, powerfully fragrant with Christ as his was—I'd let people attribute these spurious motives to me if they wanted to! I had never heard of him or his Lisu tribe before, but after ten days of watching him and listening to him, I was thoroughly convinced that he was one of God's great men. I was to learn later (and how it thrilled me!) that many of the wisest and saintliest of our times also thought that J. O. Fraser was outstanding in his generation. I was only a young girl, with just a girl's experience of life, but I knew I had touched true greatness when I met J. O. Fraser.

But there was also Dorothy Bidlake—she had been at that conference too—a missionary candidate going out for the first time. Why? Because she could not get work at home? That was not true. She was a successful secretary in the business world. Disappointed in love? Well, she surely had gotten over it, if that had been the compelling motive. Pink-cheeked, dimpled, blue-eyed Dorothy simply sparkled with vivacity and fun. No pining away around her! She was enjoying every moment of life—and not forgetting who gave it. Every memory of our times of relaxation between meetings brought a grin—how I had enjoyed Dorothy!

"No, Mother." I had weighed the evidence, and

I spoke with conviction. "That is not true in all cases, whatever it might have been in some."

"Well," wailed Mother desperately, "but you would be an object of charity! Just think of people passing the hat around for *my* daughter! I could never take the disgrace of it."

For the third time I was utterly astonished. What an interpretation to put on people's giving to the Lord's work on His far-flung battle line! And this from the president of the Women's Missionary Society! I myself had newly found the Lord, and giving to His service that others could have what I now enjoyed was a sweet joy to me. That it should be patronized and called *charity* filled me with resentment. I was too young to realize that my mother was deliberately exaggerating in order to dissuade her only daughter from leaving her side. But I fear there are too many church members who *do* have that view of giving to missions. So I would just like to record here that a gift to foreign missions with such a background motive is to me like offering a heap of sawdust. And I wonder if it is not also to the Lord! Whenever I receive a gift for personal use, one of the first reactions is joy that now I have some more tithe money to use for Him. The Lord Himself has said: "It is more blessed to give than to receive," and this is true of those who give for love of Him. But I do not know what joy sawdust-givers can get.

Anyway, here was my first obstacle to answering God's call. My mother was adamant and became hysterical if the conversation along this line continued. I was set to obey the Bible, and it said, "Honor thy father and thy mother." How could I prepare to be a missionary when my mother said it would kill her? And she would never consent.

I went to my father, who had always been an earnest lay preacher and who had offered me to God for China when I was born. Here surely I would find encouragement! But, no.

"I'm willing for you to be a missionary, but I won't help you financially," he said. "You'll have to take up Bible study somewhere. You might just as well learn to trust God for your finances *now*. Better learn such difficult lessons in America than in China. If God wants you to go, He will provide the funds apart from me. I'm not giving you a cent, so don't expect it, dear."

Of course the money matter had been a big obstacle when I first realized that to become a missionary I would need Bible training. Although I had been teaching school for more than a year, I had just finished paying off my college debt and so had no bank account. But I had enrolled as a night student at Vancouver Bible School and was working toward my goal as well as I could. It would of course take years to graduate from night school, and with the impatience of youth I longed to be through study and on my way to China—longed to begin my life-work!

But in 1924 God had already wonderfully overcome the money obstacle. It was the kind of experience you read about in storybooks, so I had to pinch myself to believe it had really happened, and that it had happened to me.

It was at The Firs Conference of 1923 that, under the appeal of Mrs. Edna Whipple Gish from South Gate, Nanking, China, I had actually surrendered for foreign service. In the school years that followed

I had enrolled in evening Bible school and, realizing how long it would take, I had begun to pray that God would help me in this matter. Without money how could I get Bible training quickly? My parents had moved to Victoria, and I was boarding in Vancouver while teaching in the Cecil Rhodes School. I had no Christian young friends whatever (God gave me a stern but enriching lesson that year in His ability to meet loneliness). The only person with whom I could ask fellowship in prayer in this matter was a middle-aged single lady missionary, retired from Formosa because of asthma. She came about once a week to pray with me and encourage me to go on in the Lord. Her name I forget—let us call her Miss F——.

In the spring of 1924 Miss Marjorie Harrison, a talented young candidate, arrived at the China Inland Mission Home in Vancouver. The oldest daughter of Dr. Norman B. Harrison, author and Bible teacher, Marjorie had looked forward to going to China for years and had saved her earnings so that she might be able to pay for her own outfit and passage. None of us expected to hear that this wonderful gifted Christian worker would be turned down by the CIM Council, but her medical examination had found her far too delicate to stand pioneer life in the Far East. The CIM knew from experience that one who had bad headaches at home would find them much intensified out in China.

Marjorie took the blow like the fine little soldier she was. For years she had lived, worked, aimed, and thought of China as her lifework. This was a shattering blow. But alone in her bedroom, after the news had been broken to her, she knelt down and made a further renunciation to Him whom she loved and served. "Dear Lord," she prayed, "this money I have saved for my outfit and passage—I dare not take it back. Will You help me to find someone to go to China in my place? I will use it for that one." No one but the Lord knew of that offering of a sweet savor, and Marjorie herself had no idea how He would work to show her who was to go in her place. But she had offered. She had accepted this disappointment as from Him, and when the supper bell rang she went down quietly and took her place at the table.

Now in the Lord's arranging, Miss F——— was a guest at the table that evening. She was the only person in the city who knew I was praying for funds to take Bible training in order to go to China. As the conversation perhaps touched on candidates and China, Miss F——— exclaimed involuntarily, "I wish Isobel Miller could go to Bible school!"

Marjorie looked up. She had met me at The Firs Conference in 1923. I was modestly dressed, and she knew I was earning a teacher's salary. She had never thought that I lacked anything.

"Why can't Isobel go?" asked Marjorie quietly. No one present knew the thought that was springing up in her heart.

"She hasn't the money," announced Miss F———. "She had a college debt to pay back, and so could not save anything. She wants to go to China, you know."

Marjorie said nothing—she was always one who did not let her right hand know what her left hand did. But after supper she inquired for my phone number, called me up, and asked me to come over and see her.

I was delighted. I had not even known that Marjorie was in the city! Merely anticipating a joyous time of fellowship with one my own age whom I had not seen for a long time, I raced happily over to the CIM home and fell on Marjorie's neck.

Soon we were alone in her bedroom and she was unfolding to me the events of that day in her life, not telling me, however, of her prayer.

I was amazed. Marjorie Harrison to be turned down by the CIM? Why, of course it must be a mistake! It could not really be a final decision! All the ignorant impetuosity of youth tumbled over my lips. I was indignant, then broken-hearted for her. I wanted to storm, to go see someone and make him change his mind, to *do something*. But Marjorie only smiled.

Then she told me of her prayer, of Miss F———'s innocently supplying the answer, and said, "So I feel the Lord has indicated that you, Isobel, are the one whom I am to send in my place. And as you are not ready to go, I will use my passage money to send you to Bible school, if you will let me."

I was dumbfounded. Not once had I foreseen such an outcome. I suppose I tried to refuse it. To use dear Marjorie's hard-earned pennies that were to have taken her to China—this would be sacrilege. And yet I had been praying for the Lord to open a way for me to train to go out as a missionary, and here was a door almost miraculously open! Dare I refuse? Was this not the hand of the Lord?

"I don't have enough money to put you through, Isobel," said Marjorie. "I would like you to go to Moody Bible Institute in Chicago. Now I have enough to pay your train fare there and your board for the first year. I have not enough to pay your way back, nor any for pocket money—your clothes, carfare, and such. You would have to trust the Lord for all that."

Well, that seemed simple. If the Lord could work so wondrously to help me the first big step, I could surely trust Him for the second and third steps.

"That is all right, Marjorie," I answered. "My biggest obstacle is my mother. She may not consent, and the Bible says to honor your parents." And so we talked together, each of us awed and blessed by the revelation of the hand of our God so fresh upon us.

It was an excited Isobel that went home that night to her lone room in the house where she boarded. I was very much awed—two girls in that big city, each not knowing the other was there: one praying to be guided as to whom to choose to go to China; the other praying for money to train to go. And God connected them by dear Miss F———.

Then Marjorie, herself a graduate of the Bible Institute of Los Angeles, had selected Moody for me. I would never have done that. A staunch Canadian, I would have chosen Toronto Bible College, if the newly opened Vancouver Bible School had been considered too small. Why Moody? So far away! Neither Marjorie nor I knew of the existence of a young man named John Kuhn. Much less did we know that he was already there. How very important it is to obey the Lord, *step by step!* We cannot know how much may hinge on one single step. The whole course of a life might be changed by just a step.

My parents, of course, were in Victoria, and I do not remember whether I wrote them my wonderful news or waited until holiday time which would give an opportunity for a face-to-face talk. Whichever it was, I was totally unprepared for my mother's excited and bitter opposition. Accept money from Marjorie? Why that was *charity!* Her daughter to live on charity, etc., etc.! Then came those amazing concepts of foreign missionaries and their support which are recorded at the beginning of this chapter.

I was in a dilemma. I had surrendered my life to the Lord and was earnestly desiring to obey Him faithfully. I felt He had called me to China Inland Mission. (I wanted to work with a group who proved God daily as Hudson Taylor had done.) I had prayed for an opportunity to train for His service, and He had so wonderfully answered. But my mother? His Word said to obey your parents. I was too young a Christian to know that when God's Word conflicts with man's word, we are committed to obey Him. He tells us to submit to civil authorities (Rom. 13:1, 2). Yet when the Sanhedrin said, "Don't preach," and God said, "Preach," the early apostles did not hesitate to disobey that civil authority (Acts 4:19). And God's blessing was on them.

Now I would like you to watch how tenderly the dear Lord worked for me in this complicated matter. Not till many years later did He show me that these crises in life may be looked upon as platforms whereon we are tried. Yes, but whereon God's power is manifested "before angels and men," and very particularly *before ourselves.*

Cornelius Vanderbreggen, Jr., once said that Philippians 3:10 (A.S.V.)—"that I may know him, and the power of his resurrection, and the fellowship of his sufferings, becoming conformed unto his death"—is *experienced* in reverse.

1. We are given a situation wherein we choose to

act as He would, that is, to be conformed to His death.

2. In that choice we shall meet with suffering—but unexpectedly discover deep, sweet fellowship with Him—the fellowship of His suffering.
3. In that situation His resurrection power will manifest itself.
4. The end of the whole matter will be that we have come to know Him, oh, so much better.

I was on the platform of obstacles. I had *chosen* to be conformed to His death. Not to smash through Mother's life in order to have my own way. Yet I chose also to obey His call. There was suffering; Mother's threat that I would go to China only over her dead body lacerated me. But the third part? Where was the power of His resurrection? The money obstacle had been met. (It was miraculous in my eyes. Never had such a thing happened to me in all my twenty-two years.) But how would He change Mother? How could He even make her willing for me to go to Moody—the very first step?

It was the close of the summer of 1924. I had returned home from The Firs Conference, where I had met Mr. J. O. Fraser and Dorothy Bidlake, and if it was to be Moody Bible Institute in the fall term I must begin to take action. I must resign teaching, for instance, at least one month before school opened—that was required by the school board. I must send in application papers to Moody Bible Institute—one did not arrive on the doorstep of an educational institution and expect to be received immediately. And I had the feeling that I should know before I made a final decision whether or not Moody Bible Institute students could work their way through school. I had no money for incidentals, not

even enough for one term's carfare. There was no
longer time to write Moody Bible Institute for information and await a reply before the deadline
when I must resign my position. Why had I been
so stupid as not to think of this long ago?

Then came a Friday morning toward the end of
July (I think it was) when I remember sitting in
the kitchen looking at these difficulties with a feeling of despair. It seemed absolutely impossible that
all these obstacles could be removed in time for
me to enter Moody in September. To obtain Mother's
consent alone was an insurmountable obstacle. How
could I find out in time if I could work my way
through Moody?

> Then comes a turn in the affairs of men
> Which taken at the tide, leads on to fortune,

said Shakespeare with his worldly wisdom.

There is a kind of spiritual counterpart of this.
When any child of God decides to step out in absolute obedience to the will of God, there will be a
frantic effort by the powers of darkness to block
him. Obstacles will spring up to hinder and discourage that one. The possibility of obedience will seem
more and more hopeless. When things are the black-
est and most discouraging is the very time *not to
give up*. That kind of namby-pamby surrender will
be quickly swamped. To keep looking at our difficulties will also swamp us. We need to look reso-
lutely away from the impossibilities and *to the
Lord*. His help will come, though often it cannot
break through to us until the last moment. It is very
important that we be ready and prepared for action
up to the last split second. God does not miss even
that split second. He may seem to be delayed, but

He will not be too late for the expectant soul waiting in active faith.

That last-possible morning, sitting in the kitchen, with the need for a final decision pressing upon me, I turned to Christ and in my heart said, "Lord, what shall I do? If I don't decide this week end I shall be compelled to teach school this fall term."

Clear as if spoken came the answer: "Speak to your mother again and use E———'s going to Moody." Now my father had forbidden me to mention China or Bible training to my mother again. Every time I had tried to broach the subject to Mother she had become hysterical and would take to her bed weeping and declaring she was ill. "She is going to become a hypochondriac if this keeps on," said my father, "and you are the cause. I forbid you to talk to her any more about these matters." So even to discuss the matter of going to Moody seemed hopeless.

Now I must explain the little matter of E———. One of my mother's "strong weaknesses" was to see me well married. That is, she had almost a mania for wanting to see me married to someone with a good education and social status in life. That very summer I had had an offer of marriage from one who seemed all Mother wanted. He was a university graduate, very brilliant, a fine Christian, felt called to the Lord's work, and came from an exceptionally fine family. I deeply respected and admired E———, but somehow just did not love him. I had not said a final no, for the offer was a complete surprise, and I had given such a thing no thought. I myself did not understand why I did not fall in love with such a fine Christian. But I did not intend to marry without love. Mother was indig-

nant and impatient with me. "You are too sentimental," she declared. "Respect is the best foundation
for marriage," and so on. Wearied with contentions,
I had just avoided mentioning E—— at all. But a
few days before this Friday morning I had received
word that E—— also planned to go to Moody Bible
Institute that September! I had not told Mother because I was so tired of arguing with her. But now
the voice had said clearly, "Speak to your mother
again and use E——'s going to Moody." Just then
Mother walked into the kitchen; so, casual outwardly,
but heart beating furiously, I said, 'I've just heard
that E—— is applying to go to Moody this fall.
Really, Mother, I don't know why you are so against
my going."

She stopped working, thought it over with surprise, then answered, "Who said I was against your
going? You can go if you like—you pay your own
expenses, that is all. We cannot help you. E—— is
a very fine young man," with much satisfaction.

I nearly jumped at that. "Mother, do you really
mean that?" (How wildly my heart beat!) "Because
if you do, I will write and resign from my school
job."

"Yes," said Mother calmly. "You can go to Moody
if you are so set on it. But I didn't say you could
go to China!"

It was just as easy as that! When God's split
second had arrived, the door swung open as if on
well-oiled hinges. Later on Mother repented this
consent, and many a stormy session ensued. But by
that time I had already resigned from my teaching
position, my bridges were burned behind me, and
there was nothing to do but go on. I might mention
too that after all, E—— did not go to Moody that

fall. His relatives counseled his taking seminary training and at almost the last moment he switched from Moody to a seminary. But at the moment when I had told Mother he was going to Moody, that had been his bona fide intention.

Now back to that Friday morning. The obstacle of Mother's consent was gone, but there still remained the question—did Moody Bible Institute allow its students to work their way through school? My faith was not sufficient to allow me to go forward confidently without knowing this beforehand. And instead of scolding me for this lack of faith, the Lord worked wonderfully and indulgently for me.

I was sitting in a chair beside the kitchen table when the thought came, *If only I knew someone in Chicago to whom I could wire this question!* The idea that I could wire the Institute itself never occurred to me. And then a very wonderful thing happened. Suddenly I realized that I was sitting on top of a couple of magazines which someone had left on that kitchen chair. Mechanically I got up and pulled them out from under me, intending to set them in their proper place, when my eye caught a notice printed on the back of the top magazine. It ran:

> Mr. and Mrs. Isaac Page have been transferred to the Chicago area. If anyone wishes to communicate with them, their address is . . . .

and there lay the full address. It was the back page of a copy of *China's Millions*. If it had fallen straight from Heaven I could not have been more startled. Daddy Page! My father's dear friend. Nine years earlier he and his wife had been about to sail for

China under the China Inland Mission, and they had taken their last homeside meal in our home. Daddy Page was so full of jokes and fun that I had loved him. But as he was saying good-by, he had placed a hand on my young shoulder and said, "Isobel, I am going to pray that God will send you to China as a missionary!" My first (unspoken!) reaction was, *You mean thing!* I had no intention of going to China and still less of being a missionary. But Daddy Page went to China, leaving a very uncomfortable little girl behind him. Years passed, years in which I had plunged into worldly gaiety and even lost my faith for awhile. Dimly I remembered hearing that Mrs. Page's health had failed, necessitating their return to America. Where they were I had no notion—now their address was right in my hand and it was—*Chicago*. It was so miraculous and so definitely an example of "Prayer is the soul's sincere desire, uttered *or* unexpressed" that I was awed, and to this day have never lost the thrill of it.

I went immediately to the telegraph office and wired something like this: IS IT POSSIBLE TO WORK ONE'S WAY THROUGH MOODY BIBLE INSTITUTE? PLEASE WIRE COLLECT. ISOBEL MILLER.

Within a matter of hours came the answer: YES, INDEED. THE INSTITUTE EVEN HAS AN EMPLOYMENT BUREAU TO HELP YOU FIND APPROPRIATE WORK. HOPING TO SEE YOU. ISAAC PAGE.

By Monday morning my resignation from school-teaching was in the post office and that bridge was burned behind me.

And now Satan got discouraged and left me alone, do you think? Ah, you do not know him! Discouragement is not allowed in the enemy's ranks—that is their favorite weapon against human beings! That last month before I was to sail for Seattle and take the train to Chicago was the keenest testing of the whole year.

Mother tried unremittingly to make me change my mind. My father had gotten into serious trouble which eventuated in litigation. Father was roent-genologist for a noted surgeon, Dr. Ernest Hall. An unprincipled young doctor in the same office build-ing, jealous of their large practice, hired false wit-nesses who charged Father with privately treating two patients, that is, practicing without the surgeon's orders. Such an offense was punishable by imprison-ment or a large fine. There had been no one else in the office at the hour Father treated these two, so it was their word against Father's and Dr. Hall's. It had been cleverly staged. Father's trial was dock-eted for the morning of the very day when I must leave for Moody.

Now that year had come word that all Father's savings, invested in two mining companies, had been lost. He had lost every cent—there would be no money to pay a fine. My brother, newly discharged from the army of World War I, was as yet unem-ployed. That left me as bread-earner in case the judgment went against Father—so ran my mother's pleading. I was an ungrateful, unconscionable child to go off and desert her at such a crisis in family history, she said, and so on, every day.

This was my suffering on my platform of obstacles. But the fellowship of the Lord was my daily strength and bolster. And how wondrously His resurrection power had worked for me and sustained me! I was sure, now, that I was in the path of His choice for me, and the experience of the past month had taught

me that final deliverance might not come until the
very last split second. So I must get ready in faith
to go through the door, so to speak, if it opened
at the last moment. That meant I must allow Marjorie to buy my ticket East. I must arrange my student's visa papers for entrance to the United States—
not to speak of my application papers. Financially
I was tested. Marjorie sent me my ticket across
country, but after I had paid my head tax I had
practically nothing left for food on the train—three
nights and two days. Well, I figured, if Moses fasted
forty days, I could fast two or three. I did not know
that I would be asked to pay a month's board in
advance as soon as I reached the Institute!

But I was the Lord's child. Levi received no
inheritance among the sons of Israel, for the Lord
was his inheritance (Deut. 10:9). My first encouragement came from such an unexpected source. I
had gone down to the boat to see Mr. J. O. Fraser
sail for China. In a moment when other friends
were looking over the ship, Mr. Fraser turned to
me and said something like this: "I have been keeping two accounts, Miss Miller. One is my personal
account and the other is for investing in the Lord's
work. I wish to close this second account before
I leave America and I find I have a few dollars
left. You are going to Moody—I do not know whether
you could use it or not."

I was astounded, but recognizing the hand of the
Lord in it I said, "Thank you, I can!" This was the
beginning of the Lord's largess.

The last painful day arrived. My boat was to leave
at half-past two in the afternoon and my father
was on trial in court that morning. I had to send
my trunk to the boat not knowing the outcome.

You can imagine the tension of those last hours. At half-past ten our phone rang. Daddy's voice came over the line, "Praise God! Fully acquitted." The Lord had vindicated my faith.

So I left on the afternoon boat for Seattle, with Mother's weeping face as my last memory. Little did I know that I was never to see her on earth again. (Just here I would like to say that Mother was really a sweet, generous woman. I feel that I failed often to be as tender with her as was her due. I was impatient that she was not more yielded to God's will. I had yet to learn the suffering, when one's affections are nailed to the cross. It was a crucifixion experience for her to be asked to give her only daughter, and she was fighting it. That was not her norm. Her neighbors and friends would all testify to the unselfishness which usually characterized Mother. It is too bad that these pages should mention her only at the time of her greatest weakness and agony.)

Before 1924 closed, Mother was in Heaven, all her tears wiped away forever. She died as the result of an operation. Of course her words of prescience recurred to me and overwhelmed me with grief for a few days. Then the Lord Himself caused an old friend of Mother's to write me a letter. This was the gist of it:

> You would like to know, I am sure, that the evening before your mother was operated on, she wrote me a long letter. In it she told me that in view of the danger of the morrow's surgery she had been reviewing her life. And she said, "I have come to the conclusion that all my busy WCTU and Women's Missionary Society work has been but wood, hay, and stubble. *I feel my little girl has chosen*

the better part in wishing to devote all her life to the Lord. If God spares me tomorrow I shall try to be different and build with gold, silver, and precious stones."

But God saw that the affectionate heart had suffered enough, so He gathered her Home to Himself where she could watch her little girl go through the dangers and vicissitudes of missionary life with full knowledge from that other side of the purpose and outcome—and so full rest. But I always felt that God *had* removed the last obstacle and that I went to China with my mother's full consent and blessing.

What a platform! Gladly would I miss the failures and faults of mine that marred its human side. But I still glory in the wonderful revelation of a tender, faithful Saviour, never deserting and never a moment too late.

It may be like an anticlimax to explain how He brought me to Chicago and started me in at the Institute with my financial needs—especially the unknown ones—fully cared for, but I would like to record it to His glory.

In Seattle I found many friends waiting to cheer me on my way. And instead of the usual box of candy, *bon voyage* gift, this one and that one slipped me a little envelope with money in it. When at last the train was speeding on its way, I found I had not only sufficient for meals on the trip, but enough to pay my first month's board in advance.

Dr. Page met me at the train and took me to the Institute. He waited while I registered and was assigned to my room, then took me for an ice-cream soda, eager to learn how the Lord had worked to answer his prayer of long ago. As I told him, tears of joy ran down his face.

"For nine years Mrs. Page and I have prayed that you would be called to China, Isobel, even through all those years when you were going in the opposite direction. I had a church in Penticton (B. C.) for awhile. I was there when you and the University Players Club came to town and I saw your name on the billboards as acting in *Mr. Pim Passes By*. I sent a note around to the theater asking to see you but got no answer. But we prayed on."

Although God had foreseen and provided for my first month's board in advance, I was not prepared for Moody's announcement that the first-semester students are not allowed to take employment. This rather staggered me, for I had need to buy some winter clothes. Chicago winters are much colder than Vancouver's, and my winter clothing was not heavy enough. Following Hudson Taylor's principles, I told no one but just went to prayer about it. When Dr. Page asked me how I was getting on, I replied, "I'll not be allowed to work the first semester—they say that is the ruling for everybody. I don't yet know what I will do."

His only comment was, "Well, we can pray about it." So the matter was left.

A couple of days later Dr. Page came again to see me. "Put on your coat, Isobel," he said. "I've got permission from the dean to take you around the corner. There is someone I want to introduce you to." Wondering what friend of his could be living in that neighborhood, but still glad for a break in school routine, I ran off gaily for my coat.

Down one block and up one block, he led me and —into a bank! Into the manager's room he walked and said to that august personage, "I wish to introduce you to Miss Isobel Miller. Here is $100.00 to open a bank account for her." I have never gotten over the shock of that moment. I stuttered and stammered and the more confused I was, the more Daddy Page grinned. (I had always called him Daddy Page.) The matter was taken care of, and out I walked with a bank book!

Of course I remonstrated, but Daddy Page answered seriously, "Your father has given me and mine as much as this and more in years gone past. This is just a small return to him—take it that way." I knew my father did things like that, so I was comforted into accepting it. But I often wondered how a poor China Inland Mission missionary could find $100.00 to give away all of a sudden like that. Maybe a relative had died and left them a legacy. Some twenty years later when on a furlough I met Dr. Page and decided to ask him. By this time, having been a CIM missionary myself for nearly two decades, I knew that that gift was really wonderful. So I reminded him of it and asked where he got it—was it a legacy?

I will never forget how he laughed! He threw back his head and just laughed till he cried. "No Isobel," he said wiping the hilarious tears away. "I remember it perfectly. We didn't have any legacy. We just emptied our bank account, that was all. We figured that we were old-timers in the life of faith and you were just beginning. It would be easier for us to trust the Lord. A legacy? Oh-ho-ho," and off he went laughing again.

So the obstacles were removed, by deep but cheerful sacrifice on the part of others. It was Marjorie's mother who told me how Marjorie went without new clothes that winter in order to pay my board bill each month, for the outfit money did not last all the first year. The next year I had the full amount to work and trust for. Emergencies came and my adventures with God in the financial realm were just as thrilling as Hudson Taylor's had been. The One who proved Himself a living Saviour to the founder of the China Inland Mission was just as living and faithful sixty years later to a little new trainee. And He will be to anyone who will surrender all to Him and step out in obedience to His call.

> Jesus, the prisoner's fetters breaks,
>   And bruises Satan's head;
> Power into strengthless souls He speaks,
>   And life into the dead.

CHAPTER TWO

UNCONGENIAL WORK

MOODY BIBLE INSTITUTE is located in an old, crowded district of Chicago to be a witness. Needless to say, great care is taken to protect its young women students, and the Employment Bureau examines the places of work to which the Institute girls are sent. Jobs of course must be part-time and at hours that do not clash with class instruction. This narrows the field of possible employment.

I was assigned as noon-hour-rush waitress in a large wholesale house. This firm had a nice restaurant for its customers, but I was not sent there. I was sent into the restaurant for its employees — a servant to the servants. The employees' restaurant was decidedly second-class and, as there were about one thousand employees all wanting lunch immediately, rush-hour help was a necessity. The regular waitresses were mostly big women, six feet tall or more. They boasted that they could carry five dinners (from soup to coffee and dessert) at one time. I staggered under two. More than that, there was a shortage of dishes, especially coffee creamers. These latter were so few that there was a continual fight behind the scenes to get possession of them — for we dared not serve an order without them. It was not our work to wash dishes but in order to get possession of a creamer, we had to grab a dirty one, wash it, then fill it. This of course delayed us. Every day there was this struggle to get hold of the needed creamers. I once had a manager swear at me and actually kick me because I was slow in filling his order — I was searching for a creamer, that was the only reason.

We all had to wear white uniforms. These were clean every day *but not mended.* The regular waitresses, arriving early, picked out the good uniforms and left the old torn ones to us rush-hour girls. Frequently I had to wear one originally intended for one of the six-footers, so of course it came down to my toes and bulged over my shoulders. "Ye are made a spectacle unto all men" was literally fulfilled. With a torn sleeve and apron of nightgown length I was literally a spectacle, but my sense of humor carried me over such a little matter. The inability to carry more than two dinner orders on one tray and the delay caused by the shortage of creamers were of much more concern.

The waitresses and the male cooks were obviously what is called a tough gang. They needed the Gospel if anyone did, but there was never any time to talk! We were truly rush-hour girls. Gradually the other waitresses became friendly, and one big strapping woman in particular used to greet me each day with a thunderous clap on the back and the hail: "How the H—— are you today, little girl?" I braced myself when I saw the big hand stretched out to come down! But it was meant for affectionate greeting. I was glad that someone felt kind toward me, and again the ludicrousness of it all brought a grin.

In the summer vacation of 1925 I went to my maternal aunt in Canada. But during the summer of 1926 I worked most of that hot season. The weather got very humid and the fumes of the kitchen were nauseating. All year I had worked there and I was tired; so the heat, the smells, and the rush began to affect me physically. There was one hot morning in July or August when I struggled into my uniform praying for strength to get through the two hours. I was feeling ill before I even started into that hot, smelly kitchen where the orders had to be filled.

Then came a moment when I was filling a coffee cup at the big boiler-like tureen. The room began to go around and I knew I was going to faint. I had a vision of falling under the open tureen, the boiling coffee streaming down on my unconscious form, so I gave a quick cry in my heart, "Lord, help me to get the tureen turned off first!" Instantly a most wonderful thing happened. I felt the Lord Himself come and stand behind my left shoulder. He put His right hand on my right shoulder and a tingle shot through me from head to foot. Healed completely, I calmly turned off the tureen and stood for half a second in deep, unspeakable worship and communion with Him. Then He was gone, and I turned to my tray. Not only had the nausea and faintness left, but a wonderful exhilaration thrilled through me. I seemed to fly rather than walk; I was lifted above all my circumstances until it seemed I was an onlooker at my own body in its ill-fitting uniform serving the tables. That exhilaration and physical refreshment lasted for days. I told no one of this experience—it was too intimate, too personal, too sacred to share with anyone.

It was no product of the imagination. I had only cried for strength to turn off the tureen, and my fainting mind certainly never pictured anything more than the mercy to faint where I would not be scalded. But much more had been given. In this uncongenial work He had revealed Himself and He had exhibited the power of His resurrection. More than thirty years have passed, but the blessing of that experience is still one of my rich treasures. Only once again did He come to me in *physical* presence, and that was in my early years in China.

I have hesitated to tell of this little experience lest it might stumble others who have never had such a thrilling manifestation. You are no less His because you have not had it. It is now more than twenty years since I myself have known His presence in this way, and yet I know He is still as close to me as He was then, and even dearer to me because I have had thirty more years of proving His love and faithfulness. Whether or not you have had such a manifestation of Him is not important. The important thing is—how are you acting? Are you bitter and resentful that you must live and work under such circumstances? Or are you asking to be conformed to His image, seeking fellowship with Him in this human suffering, watching for His resurrection power to be manifested, confident that you will know Him better when the discipline is past, and to be satisfied with that? The circumstance will pass in time, but the revelation you will receive of Himself, His love, and His power will enrich you forever.

Do not misunderstand me. I did not say you will be a better Christian afterward. I did not even say you would be a stronger Christian afterward. I do say you will be a richer one.

There was a sequel to my uncongenial employment. One day almost at closing time a lady came in and sat down, motioning for me to serve her. She was obviously high in the employment of the company and wore expensive rings. I filled her order but had to wait until she finished her meal in order to clear the table. By that time we were alone, and she spoke to me.

"Who are you?" she asked. "I've been watching you for several weeks. Always you are sweet and smiling. And," with a grimace, "I know this place. No one else is happy here—what is your secret?"

I could hardly believe my ears. Here was the opportunity I thought could never come—quiet and leisure to give a clear testimony. Of course I told her that the Lord Jesus had saved my soul and become my Life.

"I used to believe that," she answered sadly. "But no woman can go straight in this place." Being on vacation from school, I was in no hurry to return to the Institute. The result was that she once more held out her arms to Him who has vowed in no wise to cast out any soul that comes to Him. She came to see me and enrolled as a student in the evening school. And she gave me a beautiful opal ring for a remembrance.

It would be nice to tell you that *platforms* always eventuate in souls saved, but I have no authority to say that such fruit will be revealed to us. The Word says that we will be a *theatron* to men and angels. Some of our most painful platforms may have no human witness. In that case we should remember the significant words, *and angels*. I'm sure that the suffering of the saints, while its purpose is to teach us more of Himself, to develop and enrich us, also bears fruit in other lives. But that we leave with Him.

Of one thing we can be sure, our dear Lord is tenderly generous to us, even when we are on platforms of uncongenial tasks. All He needed to do was answer just what I asked—strength to remain standing until I got the coffee boiler turned off. It would have been more than I requested if He had merely strengthened me to stagger through those two hours without fainting. But what a wonderful "abundantly above" He gave! To give me an experience of His physical presence, fleeter than thought in coming! To give me that inner exhilaration which lifted me above the hot humid kitchen with its nauseating odors! Observers could see only a perspiring rush-hour girl hurrying through her tasks. They could not see the blessed fellowship with Him which was within. So we may take heart when we are tempted to pity some other child of God who seems to us to be oppressed overmuch. Remember, you cannot see the inner releases the Lord is able to give.

> Art thou sunk in depths of sorrow
> Where no arm can reach so low?
> There is One whose arms almighty
> Reach beyond thy deepest woe.
> God the eternal is thy Refuge—
> Let it still thy wild alarms—
> Underneath thy deepest sorrow
> Are the Everlasting Arms.
> Underneath thee, underneath thee
> Are the Everlasting Arms.
> —A. B. Simpson

CHAPTER THREE

SECRET CHOICES

A PLATFORM is a very public thing, and a secret choice is an extremely private, invisible thing. How then can we think of the two together? How can there be a platform of secret choice? Well, the *theatron* of II Corinthians 9:4 is any situation in which the child of God has a struggle. And a great many of these the world never sees nor even learns about. Yet the effect of that struggle often becomes noticeable to men. "Thy Father which seeth in secret shall reward thee openly" works in more matters than almsgiving. The incident to be mentioned in this chapter will reveal the compatibility of this chapter's title when the situation is in the hand of the Lord.

Again we return to the days at Moody Bible Institute. I found myself one unit of a large student body—including the evening school I believe the student body numbered a thousand. I was astonished to find that among all those young people gathered together at that time to study His Word and to train for His service, only about one hundred of them had foreign service in mind! To me it was incomprehensible. Knowing that only a small percentage of those who offer themselves for the foreign field are accepted to go, I felt that every young

Christian should at least *offer* to be a foreign missionary—give the Lord a chance to say if He wanted
him there or at home. As in the case of Marjorie
Harrison, many earnest souls must stay at home—
they are enough to minister to the home needs. It
would be so easy for the Lord to keep them at home;
but it is impossible for the Lord to push any out.
He has made this rule for Himself—He will compel
no man's love or obedience. How can you know
He does not want you in the far-flung battle line *if
you do not offer?* I still believe that this is the reasonable attitude to take.

Though I found a meager hundred of fellow
students who were like-minded with me in this matter, I did find very choice souls among them. I
received more blessing through the devotion and
fire of my fellow students at Moody than I did
even through my studies. I thank God for them.
After graduation we scattered, and many I did not
see again for twenty or thirty years. But when we
did meet, what a joy to find their passion for Christ
brimming over as fervently as in student days! And
what a thrill to hear from their lips that *the dreams*
of student days had been fulfilled by a gentle, kind
Master! He had inspired our dreams and His call-
ings had been justified.

But the Institute schedule was a busy one, especially for us who had to work our way through.
There came a day when the president of our Student
Volunteer band came to me exercised in soul. I
was scheduled to speak at our next meeting, and
he had a burden to lay upon my heart. "It is so easy,
with required hours of Bible reading, to let one's
own devotional time slip. And it inevitably leads to
staleness of soul. I feel that some of us are in

danger of drifting into an empty form of relationship to Him, of missing the vital personal touch each day. Will you pray, Isobel, and ask the Lord for a solution? And give us a talk on it next meeting?" I accepted the burden, and waited on the Lord. I had felt that danger myself. For certain classes we had to read a book of the Bible through—perhaps several times. Why read it again for quiet time? Especially when leisure hours were at a premium. But reading the Scriptures for a scholarly grasp of the general argument in a book, and reading it in the Lord's presence, asking Him to speak a word on which to lean that day—those were two different things. One was no substitute for the other. Yet I knew also that some students were trying to let classwork reading do for personal quiet time. Deadness of soul was inevitable.

As I prayed about it, I felt a need to gird up our loins and form a habit of putting the Lord first each day. Habit can be a wonderful ally, but it can also be a formidable foe. We ourselves can choose which kind of habits to form. My attention was drawn to II Chronicle 29:11: "My sons, be not now negligent: for the Lord hath chosen you [me] to stand before him, to serve him, and that ye [I] should minister unto him, and burn incense." Using this text for exhortation, I suggested our making a covenant with the Lord to spend one hour a day (for about a year) in the Lord's presence, in prayer or reading the Word. The purpose was to form the habit of putting God in the center of our day and fitting the work of life around Him, rather than letting the day's business occupy the central place and trying to fix a quiet time with the Lord somewhere shoved into the odd corner or leisure moment.

I had drawn up a paper with the above text and covenant promise, and asked how many would sign with me. I suggested we meet together once a month to confess any failures and to worship the Lord together.

It was a very small meeting, as it happened, and only nine signed that original covenant. I still have that piece of paper, and the reader will be interested to know that one of the nine names was John B. Kuhn.

It was never my thought that this covenant become *law*. My thought was merely to deliberately form a habit which would allow the Lord to speak personally to us all the days of our lives. Although only nine signed up that first day, somehow news of it spread, and others began to join. Then—it seems as if some human beings always have to go to extremes—some signed a covenant binding them to this hour a day *for life*. I did not sign it. What about days of illness or emergency, when it might be impossible to keep an hour quietly? There was no need *to vow;* there was only need to *form a habit* of putting God first. The hour, we agreed, could be broken up into two half-hour periods, or any division needed.

The Lord blessed us. Our monthly prayer meetings to testify and encourage one another became times of wonderful fellowship in the Lord. They grew and grew in numbers. Testimonies were often funny. One fellow at a summer camp in desperation got into a canoe and pushed out into the middle of the lake—and had a blessed time. And so on. Needless to say we kindled one another. Ten years later, on our first furlough, we visited the Institute and found that this prayer group was still going on, though no

one remembered when it got started or what was
the origin. We did not enlighten them, but gloried
in the work of the Spirit.

To keep my hour-a-day required planning. At
half-past six each morning I was due in the dining
room to set tables. I tried getting up at five, but
my health began to fail. After various efforts I found
I could maintain normal weight if I arose at half-
past five. But go where to be alone? My roommate
slept through until nearly breakfast time and might
resent a light at such an early hour. The only place
I could find where I would disturb no one was the
cleaning closet! So each morning I stole down the
hall, entered the closet, turned the scrubbing pail
upside down, sat on it, and with mops and dust rags
hanging around my head, I had a precious half-hour
with the Master. The other half-hour had to be
found at the end of the day.

This is the background of my platform of secret
choices. It was the evening of the Junior-Senior
party. I was a Junior and had been asked to lead
the devotional with which all such parties closed.
I was also on the program as Grandma in a Dutch
scene, off and on all through the banquet. The week
before had been so full of work and study that I
had not one moment to sit down and prepare a devotional. Work in the restaurant had delayed me, and
I arrived at the supper half-hour, hungry, exhausted,
and without any devotional prepared. Besides this,
I still had half an hour due on my quiet time!
After the party we Juniors had to clean up, and I
would not get to my room till midnight—the day
would be gone.

Here was my platform of secret choices. That supper half-hour. (1) Should I go down and eat my

supper? (2) Should I skip supper and try to prepare the devotional message? (3) Should I put God first and give that half-hour to Him? The supper bell rang, and my roommate left for the dining room. I stood for a moment irresolute; then, throwing myself on my knees by my bedside I sobbed out in a whisper, "O dear Lord, I choose Thee!" Then again, as I just lay in His presence too weary to form words, the sense of His presence filled the room. As before, the weariness and faintness all left me. I felt relaxed, refreshed, bathed in His love. And as I half knelt, half lay there, saying nothing, but just loving Him, drinking in His tenderness, *He* spoke to me. Quietly, but point by point, He outlined for me the devotional message I needed to close that evening's program. It was an unforgettable experience and an unforgettable lesson. *Putting Him first always pays.*

> Lord of my merry cheers,
>   My grey that turns to gold,
> And my most private tears
>   And comforts manifold,
>   *'Tis wonderful to me*
>   *That I am loved by Thee.*
>   —A.C.

In the exhilaration of that wonder I ran down to the banquet hall (or rather the hall behind it), slipped into my costume, and went through the program. At the end, when the devotional message was needed, I gave very simply what He had told me during supper hour. Such a quiet hush came over that festive scene that I knew He had spoken, and I was content.

More than twenty years passed. I was home on

furlough and visiting the Institute. It was the day of the Junior-Senior party and a group of us were reminiscing. "One Junior-Senior party always stands out in my memory," said one. "I forget who led it but it was a Dutch scene and the devotional blessed my soul. I've never forgotten it." She had indicated the date, so I knew. I was thrilled through and through. Of course I did not spoil it by telling her who led that devotional. In God's perfect workings, the instrument is forgotten. It is the blessing of Himself that is remembered.

This is how *secret* choices can become *public*. The choice and the struggle are not publicized—but the release of His resurrection power which comes to you on each platform is felt by others, and in that sense there is an audience. We may never know who this "audience" might be, but we do know that He gives us far more than we deserve.

> Christ, the Lord's Anointed, reigning
> O'er the life He died to win,
> Daily shall reveal more fully
> His great power, without, within.
> What thou never could'st accomplish
> Shall His Spirit work through thee
> While thy soul this witness beareth:
> 'Tis not I, but Christ in me.
> —F. H. ALLAN

CHAPTER FOUR

CROSSED NATURE

Now that you have read of the wonderful things the Lord did for me, I fear lest some might casually think that I myself must have been a wonderful Christian to be worthy of such blessings. I must hasten to correct this easy error. I was *not* a wonderful Christian but very much "of the earth, earthy." God's blessings are not reserved for those who are worthy; they are lavishly poured out on very unworthy ones, upon those who in their innermost souls are reaching out for Him.

I have pondered the affairs of two men, David and Ahithophel. Once they were close, dear friends. Ahithophel's counsel was so wise it was like the Oracles of God. They went to the House of God together to worship. Then David sinned. Bathsheba was Ahithophel's granddaughter. Oh, what horrible sin—adultery and then the murder of Uriah! No wonder Ahithophel was estranged and angry! Either of those sins would have scandalized him, let alone both. Surely God will bless Ahithophel and not David.

But look beneath the surface. When the prophet Nathan faced David, David repented immediately. "I have sinned," he cried. And from then on, groaning under the punishment which his sins sent him,

David still reached out in brokenhearted repentance to the Lord. "Cast me not away from thy presence," he cried (Ps. 51:11).

Ahithophel? He became like the elder brother of Christ's parable of the Prodigal Son. He refused to open his heart to God's grace of forgiveness, so his heart became filled with cold fury. He who had despised David's adultery counseled the same sin to David's son (II Sam. 16:21). He who had furiously criticized David for taking Uriah's life ended up by taking his own (II Sam. 17:23). So man proves he is really no better than the sinner he is so quick to condemn, and whom he refuses to forgive.

If Ahithophel had allowed God to melt his heart in forgiveness, the day would have come when Ahithophel would have seen Solomon, son of his granddaughter Bathsheba, upon the throne of David. And that great-grandson—looking at it from the merely human viewpoint—inherited Ahithophel's own wisdom. God blessed the sinner who opened his heart to correction, and God's blessing was lost to the sinner who closed his heart to the pleadings of grace and refused to forgive.

We do not receive His blessings then because we deserve them, but only when we obey His tender injunction, "Open thy mouth wide and I will fill it."

I had a greedily wide mouth; but if it had been wider, I might have received more.

In October, 1928, when I sailed for China, there were eight or ten of us young women who sailed together. And on that ship were Miss Ruth Paxson and Miss Ethel Davis, also going to China. Miss Paxson's book, *Life on the Highest Plane,* was then in manuscript form, and she kindly consented to give us girls an hour's Bible teaching every day while the trip lasted. Those were memorable hours! One sentence I never forgot. Standing in front of us, an experienced missionary, she looked into our faces searchingly and said, "Girls, when you get to China, all the scum of your nature will rise to the top." I was shocked. Scum? Wasn't that a strong word? All of us were nice girls—weren't we? Scum? A bit extravagant, surely. And so I was totally unprepared for the revolt of the flesh which was waiting for me on China's shores. The day was to come when on my knees in the Lord's presence I had to say: "Lord, *scum* is the only word to describe me."

I went to China eager and hopeful to be a soulwinner. I was ridiculously, pathetically unprepared for the cost. It is true that I had expected poverty and had even tried to discipline myself for it. While teaching school I had chosen a boarding house that was drab and plain, with no rugs or carpets. Fond of chocolates, I decided not to buy any candy for a year at least. This puny "self-discipline" makes me laugh now. And makes me wonder how I could have been so unprepared for the ordinary missionary hardship. I do not know, but it was so.

The China Inland Mission, true to its name, reached out to the unworked interior of that great land, where by far the great majority of unevangelized Chinese were country peasants, poor people who toil and labor in mud hovels and know nothing of the luxuries of hot baths with soap, or frequent change to clean clothing. I had to learn that it costs money to be clean; I had always taken cleanliness for granted, just like sunshine.

And so, after a happy time at language school, I found myself on a country station in a farming district, with thousands of Chinese peasants in all

directions who had never been told that Christ died
for their salvation. What a wonderful opportunity!
In spirit I reached out eagerly toward them and
then—the flesh revolted.

As in all eastern lands, and among our own poor
also, these toiling people had vermin on their persons, in their homes, and in the dust of their mud
floors. Fleas jumped on me from those floors and
nibbled joyfully. There are some people (my husband is one) whom insects are slow to attack.
Others, like myself, seem to be an open invitation
to come feast! Sitting close to a country woman,
I was likely to carry away a louse. And when asked
to spend a night in these homes, bedbugs walked
out in regiments upon me, not to speak of the air
force—flies and mosquitoes.

Their customs were different. They had no plumb-
ing in their homes, so dogs acted as scavengers.
My first experience of one particular custom so
revolted me that I could not eat my breakfast and
had to start a long journey with an empty stomach.

The food of the Chinese poor is different from
that of the middle classes, and I did not find it
palatable at first. The story of how I learned to eat
beancurd is a family joke now. My husband says,
with eyes twinkling, "You have to cry first—then you
learn to enjoy it!"

And the lack of privacy. I always had a room to
myself at home and unconsciously was fond of being by myself—a student notion I suppose. To be
thronged with people hour after hour exhausted
me emotionally, and of course a woman cannot bathe
without some kind of privacy.

The constant traveling too was a source of irri-
tation. I never did like change; I liked to get well

rooted into one comfortable spot and stay there. So the flesh was offended on every hand, and it revolted.

My husband did not seem to mind these things; so I put it down to a different disposition. Insects did not readily attack him; brought up on strong German cheeses, he did not mind if the meat served us had spoiled. He rather liked a tangy flavor! And as for crowds, he loved them. Did not like to be alone! And traveling was nectar to him; he was never happier than when on a trip.

I had been well taught in the truth of identification with Christ. I knew that these daily irritations and disagreeable things were opportunities to die to the flesh and sin. I frantically reckoned myself dead (Rom. 6:11), still I was hindered. At a God-given impulse to put my arm around some poor old woman, the flesh would inwardly shriek, "Watch out! You'll get a louse." Everywhere selfishness and self-pity would raise their ugly heads. I knew now that the scum had risen to the surface, and only the Lord could take it away.

It was during my first term of service that Amy Carmichael's books were sent to me. I was thrilled with them, recognized her high standards as Christ's own, but was appalled at my own low level of living. In fact, her books discouraged me, for *she* never seemed to have any faults! This is the reason I am recording this chapter: to register the Lord's patience and faithfulness to one who was not naturally heroic.

Amy Carmichael said quite casually, "Everything personal had gone long ago"—meaning that the self-life was under her feet before she even began her work at Dohnavur. She had terrific battles, but they were with Satan, the Lord's own antagonist. Anything so elementary as selfishness never seems to have troubled her. So I would get discouraged and put her books on the shelf saying, "You're too high for me. I cannot attain that." But they fascinated and lured me. Even when they were shelved, the sight of them would send a rapier-thrust into me:

> Let me not sink to be a clod;
> Make me Thy fuel, Flame of God!

That was really what I wanted too—I didn't want to be a clod. I would fall on my knees and weep before the Lord, asking for His help. And never did He spurn me. He was firm in correcting me but always loving. I have never attained the place where one is beyond the temptations of self. But I want to testify to what God can do to *change* a human being, one that found she was indeed—scum.

I was delighted one day when He drew my attention to Galatians 2:8: "For he that wrought effectually in Peter . . . the same was mighty in me." Paul is not discussing victory over self in this verse, but the Lord was when He pointed it out to me! Peter had lots of self-life to battle, and Paul was not entirely without his also. But He that wrought effectually in Peter was mighty also *in me*.

He had to first bring me to the place where I was so exercised in spirit over producing so little fruit for Him that nothing else mattered. Physical comforts did not matter if only souls could be born into His kingdom. Moreover, He brought me to the place where I was willing that the instrument He used be someone else if necessary. I was willing not to be the one used, if only He would permit me to see that souls *were* being born into His kingdom. Shortly after I surrendered that, He swung me into

Lisuland where I felt "at home" for the first time in China.

And He even tenderly showed me little ways to make it easier for the flesh. Insect powders helped a bit against those tiny pests, and He showed me other ways to overcome. Some of the changes He wrought in me are even funny. Here is one.

When we were first married we were invited one hot June day to dinner at a poor Christian's home. The flies were innumerable, the hut as usual like a junk shop, and through the open door came the odors of the nearby pigsty. Into such a setting brings mine hostess a dish of large chunks of boiled pork fat! Not a bit of lean. My stomach turned over. "Oh, John," I whispered, "do I have to eat this? I'll vomit sure." With a gracious nodding smile of thanks to our hostess, John deliberately picked up a big white chunk and placed it in my rice bowl as if it were the dish delectable. At the same time he said in English, "When her back is turned, give it to the friend under the table." A mangy, mongrel dog (flea-laden for sure) had pressed up against my feet several times, so I knew whom he meant. I pushed some rice into my mouth, and at a moment when she was not looking, I tilted the chunk of fat below the table. A succulent licking of chops from below testified to the joy with which my offering was received! But believe it or not, "He who was mighty in me" gradually gave me a real liking for pork fat—considered a choice dish among the Lisu as well as the country Chinese. It took time, of course, and cooler weather! But I found it a good lubricant for the dry rice and still drier steamed corn of Lisuland, and in time learned to welcome it eagerly! I enjoyed its flavor.

My dislike for traveling was changed too. I learned to look for the beauties of God in the scenery of which Yunnan, and especially Lisuland, are so rich they are like the borderland of Heaven. Always a passionate lover of beauty, I was given wonderful opportunities to adore God's thought as revealed in His creation. I keep a five-year diary, and very often in looking back I have been in a different spot each year on a given day, so frequent and full of change was my life. Yet it has been joyous and filled with happy memories. He who wrought effectually in Peter was mighty also in me. And He will be in you too.

> Across the will of nature
> Leads on the path of God.

But we do not need to fear. He does not desert us when our old Adam nature must be crossed. Some, like Amy Carmichael, get it under their feet early. Others, like myself, try His patience painfully, but that patience never gives way, and it never deserts. He that wrought effectually in Peter will be mighty also in you.

> If e'er I go astray
>   He doth my soul reclaim,
> And guides me in His own right way,
>   For His most holy name.

And always He will relentlessly hold you to His highest. He wants your soul not only purged and clean, but with a bloom upon it. Oswald Chambers calls it *the bloom of the touch of the Lord*. He says: "The true character of the loveliness that tells for God is always unconscious. Conscious influence is priggish and unchristian. If I say—'I wonder if I am of any use,' I instantly lose the bloom of the touch of the Lord."

George Matheson has a keen and discriminating word on how this bloom, this unself-consciousness is best obtained. He says, "I hear thee speak of the forgetfulness of self. Yes, my soul, but the solemn question is the *manner* of thy forgetting. How wouldst thou forget; shall it be by death or shall it be by life? Thou canst forget thyself by chloroform; but that is not greatness; it is the unconsciousness purchased by dying.

"But I know of an unconsciousness purchased by living—living in the life of another; it is the thing called love. The branch could forget itself by being withered; it prefers to forget itself by being in the vine."

He that wrought effectually in Peter will continue to work in us until He has formed in us that unconsciousness of self *purchased by living*—that bloom of the touch of the Lord! For the love of Him, our life lost in His. Lead on, O precious Christ!

CHAPTER FIVE

FRUSTRATIONS

I HAD NEVER FELT CALLED to the Chinese people, although I learned to love them when I got to know them. I had felt called to the group named China Inland Mission because they followed Hudson Taylor's principles of proving God: "Learn to move man, through God, by prayer alone."

But when I heard J. O. Fraser speak about the Lisu tribe at The Firs Conference in 1924, I had a longing to go to them. I fell in love with them! Mr. Fraser was secretly disappointed, I always felt, that that conference where he had poured out his heart brought only one volunteer for the Lisu, and that a girl! He was polite, of course, but not encouraging. It was not a woman's job; he himself had never married because he felt no woman should be asked to endure such a life.

On returning to China, to his amazement and ours, Mr. Fraser was not sent back to the Lisu tribe— he never got back to them as just their missionary. Mr. Hoste (Hudson Taylor's successor as general director of the CIM) had plans for higher leadership. He had been watching the godliness, shrewd insight, and brilliant ability of this young electrical engineer, and coveted his influence for more than just one of China's tribes. Mr. Fraser was at least fifty years ahead of his time in his vision of the indigenous church; and his deep prayer life and abandoned consecration appealed much to our general director.

But although Mr. Fraser himself did not go back to Lisuland, my call never wavered. And yet I did not dare name it a call. It was just a great longing to go to them. At Moody Bible Institute I had heard missionary challenges that drew me breathless to the edge of my seat. Especially when L. L. Legters appealed for the Indians of South America; I wished I were two people, one of whom could go to those neglected Indians. But I never wavered in the vision for the Lisu tribe—that came first. And yet, when at last I got to China and to Yunnan, the person who stood most in my way was Mr. Fraser himself! By that time I was engaged to marry John Kuhn. But I had held John off until I knew that the Mission had designated him to the tribes of Yunnan! John himself had felt drawn to the work in the far Northwest, but when the Mission assigned him to the Southwest and to the tribes, it seemed to indicate that God Himself had set His seal on our marriage. So we became officially engaged.

Mr. Fraser had had to come down to Shanghai during the antiforeign uprising of 1927 and there he met John Kuhn and—loved him. He even wrote me a letter, advising me to choose John! (He knew someone else was a possibility.) By the time John was appointed to Yunnan, Mr. Fraser had become superintendent of that province. An indefatigable language student himself and a brilliant linguist, Mr. Fraser was thrilled at John's progress in Chinese. He began, even that early, to plan that John would some day be his assistant superintendent. There was the assignment to the tribes, but all tribal workers had to study Chinese first. Mr. Fraser saw to it that

John had ample opportunity to get Chinese thoroughly.

By the time I had finished the prescribed Chinese language examinations and normally could have been sent to the tribes, Mr. Fraser delayed us, saying, "Isobel is not strong enough physically to endure such a hard life." Quite possibly my difficulties in adjusting to the squalor of peasant life—many other young workers simply took those hardships with joy—was at the back of his thinking. But I honestly think it was more that he did not want John to lose any of his prowess in Chinese. To learn the Lisu language, John would necessarily get a bit rusty in the previous language learned.

John himself was happy with either designation. He was willing to go to Lisu—he had made one trip into the Upper Salween Canyon which thrilled him—but he also enjoyed working with the Chinese. It was only John's wife who kept timidly bringing up this matter of the Lisu! Ten years had passed. It was 1924 when I first felt called to the Lisu and now it had dawned 1933 and we were still in Chinese work. The normal time for our furlough was approaching: John had been out seven years and I five years—seven was the normal term.

Had I been called to the Lisu? Or had it been just a sentimental attraction? Desperately I took it to the Lord—blessed refuge for all troubles. One could tell Him things one would be ashamed to tell another. "I guess, Lord," I whispered mournfully, "I will just have to conclude that I mistook Your guidance, and it was not a call after all."

Another application to Mr. Fraser had just brought the answer, "Wait until after your furlough. We will see then."

It was that spring that I had felt so discouraged
with my own ministry. We had opened the beautiful little plain of Yungping to the Gospel. It was
mainly Moslem in population and had not been fruit-
ful. I had worked faithfully. There was not a hamlet
or a village on that whole plain where I had not
personally gone, driven off their various dogs,
pushed my way into their dirty courtyards and
presented my message. The women were kind and
everyone was nice to me but only a mere handful
of people had accepted Christ. And most of these
were very poor illiterate women—too weak to call
a church. It was at Yungping that I told the Lord
that I would be willing to be put on the shelf, willing not to be the one He used, if only I might see
Him work!

As Lisu work seemed impossible before furlough
we mentally accepted the fact. We were expecting
a little playmate for our two-year old Kathryn. It
was then, when hope was dead, that the Lord
wrought so wondrously. But it appeared a catastrophe at first glance.

In August, 1933, John went out on a long trip
to discover what tribes inhabited an area we called
the Triangle. Kathryn and I, with three young lady
workers, were left behind in Yungping—apparently
quite safe from danger. Then one day, without warning, the Yungping River flooded. It rose so silently
that we were not aware of what was happening
until it had almost reached the level of our downstairs room. Then began a scramble to move people
who lived there to the upstairs. I was called upon
to help lift one of Miss Embery's trunks to a place
of safety, and humanly speaking, that did it. I suffered a miscarriage.

It was impossible to contact John, there being no post office in the mountain villages where he was. So it was not until he returned that he learned there was no baby to look forward to. I felt the loss more keenly than he perhaps, and as he turned to comfort me he said, "God must have some purpose in this, dear. We will just ask Him what it is."

Within twenty-four hours a letter from Mr. Fraser was in our hands. "I want your prayers for a perplexing problem," he wrote. Then he told us of the two Lisu churches in the Upper Salween Canyon which had come into being through the sacrificial pioneering of four Lisu evangelists. That trail-blazing had cost the life of one of the four.[1] Now those two little churches were flourishing, but they were six days' journey apart and there was only one missionary couple to care for the two. Mr. Fraser had written that Leila and Allyn Cooke had separated, Allyn to care for the Luda church and Leila left in charge of the Oak Flat church. "But I cannot allow this to go on," wrote our perplexed superintendent. "Leila Cooke is very brave to stay all alone in that isolated rough place, but I cannot allow husband and wife to continue in separation! Yet I have no one else to send."

John and I looked at one another—the meaning of the Lord was now clear to us. With a newborn infant it would have been well nigh impossible for us to begin such a rough life. But our two-year-old would have a wonderful time on those wooded slopes, with someone to watch her.

John and I knew now why God had taken the baby from us. We wrote to Mr. Fraser immedi-

[1] See *Nests Above the Abyss,* by the same author.

ately, told him of my accident and of our firm
belief that it was the Lord guiding us to go to
the Upper Salween.

Our dear superintendent was too much of a man
of God not to recognize the hand of the Lord. But
his common sense still held to it that my health
could not stand Lisuland.

"Go in for a trip," he wrote. "That will relieve
Mrs. Cooke's present stress over this opium persecution. John must interview the official and claim
gently the religious freedom of this land. Isobel can
judge from this trip whether she could stand it.
And as Leila Cooke has not seen another white
face for months, she will no doubt be overjoyed
to have Isobel's company."

This was the reason for our trip into the Upper
Salween in March, 1934, when Mark and other
Christian Lisu friends from Goomoo fought their
way over the snowy mountain and arrived the day
after we did!

I was thrilled with Lisuland—by the Lord's work
in salvation and by His work in creation. The Cookes
lived in a flimsy bamboo Lisu shanty. But Allyn
Cooke had worked and prepared a flourishing garden—beets, carrots, tomatoes, and such good food
grew in abundance. Leila Cooke had brought an
iron cooking-stove and a little heater, so though
life was primitive in style, it was cozy. At that time
they were living in Pine Mountain Village and had
a site on the mountainside to themselves.

The squalor and insects of poverty and primitive
living were as bad or worse than among the Chinese
farmers. But to me it was much easier to endure
for two reasons—beauty and privacy were obtain-
able. In the Chinese peasant village you were shut

up to ugly drabness. If you tried to leave the village, you found yourself in their flat rice fields, where of course you could not sit down and were very conspicuous. In Lisuland the villages were also smelly and ugly, but you could stand anywhere and lift up your eyes to the most magnificent Alpine panoramas on which to feast your soul. And for privacy there were those great mountain slopes, dotted with trees, beautiful wild flowers, and picturesque rocks. In ten minutes you could be quite alone, out of sight and surrounded by breath-taking beauty. On rainy days there was the beauty of cloud-wreathed peaks.

Living conditions in tribesland were much more difficult than on the Chinese plain. There were no stores in which to buy food or furniture. The Lisu did not use furniture. A raised plank for a bed, yes. Rough cupboards or baskets to store grain, yes. That was about all. When we moved into Oak Flat district very few Lisu used tables. They ate off a board placed on the unwashed floor (which was also the roof of the cattle pen built beneath the hut). After seeing our table, many of them began to make tables for themselves; but many were the meals which I ate off the floor, before they awakened to the possible luxury of something better. I remember one occasion when we were thus eating, the family cat made dashes for our meat dish. Being on our level—on the floor—she was very successful. But Lucius, a Lisu brother who was with us, put an end to her depredations. He caught her, held her tail down with his heel a good yard off, and placidly went on eating. Pussy yowled frantically, but no more meat was lost!

So it was that we wrote Mr. Fraser again, quite

confident that I could stand it and would love it.
Mr. Fraser replied gratefully that we might move
into Lisuland until our furlough. (John was in his
tenth year and I in my eighth when we finally left
for America.)

How thrilled we were! Frustrations last for a
time, but the will of the Lord reigns in the end—
I told myself jubilantly. It was exactly ten years
since I had first felt the call to Lisu work. Ten
years of waiting and frustration—why? Most probably because I myself had not been ready before.
I needed the hard years of plodding, which resulted
in little fruit, to make me so hungry for saved souls
that the physical hardships would not matter. In
other words, the Lord had to train me to appreciate
what He was doing among that barefooted mountain tribe before He dared let me share in the work.
I always said that Lisu work was physical hardship but spiritual luxury. The physical hardship was
obvious to anyone. It was spiritual luxury I would
not have recognized if I had gone right into Lisu
work without those barren years among the Chinese
peasants.

There had been some souls saved among the Chinese, but they were illiterate! Old women could
never read their Bible, and how is one to grow
spiritually without feeding on the Word? (In those
early years I did not know about the Chinese pho-
netic.) In Lisuland they were illiterate too, but
the Fraser Script was so simple and easy that a
bright lad could learn to read in one month! Then
you can begin to open the Scriptures to that one.
I had to learn to appreciate that! That is a luxury.
We were so isolated, and living conditions were
so hard that the "isms" did not come near us. No

Roman Catholic or Seventh-day Adventist offering your new convert clothes or other enticements to get him away from you—that is a luxury. The Holy Spirit blowing like a strong wind across the mountains, new converts springing up in this village and in that one—that is a luxury. Others had paid the painful price of pioneering—we merely walked into the blessing. And the Lisu with a little training could sing in parts! Oh, how my soul had been galled by the monotone singing of the Chinese peasant! This glorious love of music and keep aptitude for it was a luxury. And so on.

Those ten long years of waiting and frustration had been needed to open my eyes to the privileges of being allowed to share in the Lisu work. If I had gone into the work as soon as my Chinese language exams were passed, I would have taken the tide of blessing for granted, the young converts eager to be taught as the usual thing, and I might have chafed at the physical hardships—the poor and monotonous food, the difficulty of getting help and getting supplies and so on. My spiritual eyesight needed to be clarified.

After permission was given to move, we were frustrated again! John took sick. Amoebic dysentery first, and then a hernia operation. Why, oh why? "It must be the Devil"—my irritated flesh wanted to blame someone, and the Devil is always a handy object. Medical attention was needed, and the new worker just arrived at Tali was a doctor—Dr. Stuart Harverson. So to Tali we repaired.

Here we met this new missionary who had come from a cultured well-to-do home, yet who accepted the physical hardships not just with patience, but with zest! Doc, as we called him, simply plunged

into life among the peasants with joy and abandon-
ment. He was a living rebuke (though unconscious
of it) to my shrinking horror of vermin, dirt, and
bad smells. And the Lord mightily blessed. As John
was sick in bed, and Doc had not yet learned Chinese,
I had to go with him on medical calls to act as interpreter. In a few weeks I saw many Chinese
saved; as many in four weeks as I had in the whole
previous year. (It was not a Moslem community
like Yungping; still, God taught me a lesson.)

In December, 1934, we were at last ready and
allowed to move into Lisuland, taking over the district of Oak Flat.[2]

My pen is tempted to dwell on those happy days,
but this is the story of frustrations, and I must pur-
sue the theme.

Every summer in Lisuland comes the rainy season. It had been necessary for us to leave comfortable Pine Mountain Village and rebuild the shanty
in Oak Flat Village. Our house site was beautiful—
at the edge of a precipitous drop where no other
shanties could be built, giving us a bit of privacy.
But the garden space had been a landslide and was
simply gravel. We were not good gardeners like
Allyn Cooke and, added to that, the soil was rocky,
so our vegetable garden was a failure. Leila Cooke
had joined her husband in the Luda church six
days' journey away, so we had no senior workers
to advise or counsel us. We saw the need of visiting in the villages, staying a week in a place and
teaching the Christians. We had to speak in Chinese
at first, Lisu Evangelist John or Job interpreting for
us, while at the same time we tried to learn their
language. Traveling in the rainy season and living

[2]Told in *Precious Things of the Lasting Hills* (out of print).

in leaky Lisu huts are dangerous to the health—we never tried that again! But that first summer in our ignorance, we did.

When little Kathryn took ill with a very high, strange fever I wrote Dr. Harverson, our nearest medic, for advice, but it was two months before his prompt answer arrived! The Burma Road had not been built in those days.

In August John decided to make a trip into Burma to visit the beloved Goomoo group of Christians, whom no white missionary had ever met. That meant he would be gone about a month (seven days' journey each way) while Kathryn and I stayed home at Oak Flat. John took Teacher John and left Teacher Job with me, so each of us had a Lisu who could speak Chinese and act as our interpreter. So we parted.

Unknown to us I had picked up a germ of erysipelas on our last trip among the Lisu, and John was no sooner out of reach and communication than I became ill with strange symptoms. I had never even seen, almost never heard of erysipelas. I just knew I was ill and running a fever. I couldn't get up. Dear Homay took care of little Kathryn, who preferred Lisu food to our American food, so she was not a worry, but I could not eat. Rice, corn, pumpkins, beans—they did not appeal. Homay kept apologizing, said it was famine year, and she could not get meat or even eggs. Powdered milk we had, and some canned meat. But I was soon too ill to know what I should have had. Never can I forget the tender concern of the dear Lisu. Job came many times a day and offered to go for help to Paoshan where the China Inland Mission had stationed a young nurse, Kathleen Davies, with Winifred Embery. But I said no, no, Job must not disturb them. It was a rough six days to get to them; it would take several days to purchase supplies, hire carriers and pack to come. Two weeks? I'd be better then! No, I said to him, just wait and pray.

Dear Job got more anxious as I grew weaker. One morning he appeared with some oil. He anointed me according to James 5:17 and prayed over me, then sang, "The Great Physician Now Is Near." I was deeply touched by his love, but singing was not Job's strong point, and I'm afraid I chuckled after he left over the memory of that croaking effort. Still I did not get better.

Then one morning Homay walked in and announced, "Teacher Job has gone, Ma-ma! He got up at four o'clock this morning and has gone to Paoshan to bring medical help for you."

"Oh, dear," I thought dismally. "Now Mr. Fraser will say, 'I told you so. Isobel in Lisuland only eight months and medical help has to be called for!' Oh, dear!" But I was getting too weak to care. My worst discomfort was my unwashed condition. The fever made me perspire, and I had been too weak to wash myself for days. I called dear Homay and tried to explain to her what a bed-bath was. She listened incredulously, dubiously, but did her best. Soon she was back with a basin of hot water. She set it down beside the bed, dipped her plump brown hands in it, and proceeded to stroke me! That was the most she had comprehended. She knew she was not being successful and looked so grieved and anxious that I had to pretend to be satisfied in order to comfort her. I do not remember much of what happened after that.

I was told later that Job ran his feet into blisters and did the six days' journey in four. But with all that painful effort it was more than two weeks before he was able to bring the girls into our village. The girls could not walk those mountains, so mountain-chair coolies had to be found, and not everyone wanted to carry on those Salween heights! The girls guessed, and rightly, that I was sleeping on boards, so they decided to bring a folding camp bed. This with other comforts had to be carried, and carriers had to be found. Job chafed at the delay these preparations took, but at last the party climbed the last mountain and reached Oak Flat Village.

It was a wonderful moment for me when my bones felt the softness of that camp bed. But I was so weak that I collapsed when Nurse Kathleen tried to give me a bed-bath. "This is not from erysipelas," she said, puzzled. "This is semistarvation. Homay, bring me some eggs!"

"Sorry, Make-Medicine-Lady," answered that dear girl anxiously, "but there aren't any."

"Well, kill a chicken and we will make some broth."

Again Homay's face fell. "There aren't any chickens, Make-Medicine-Lady. This is a famine season, and no one has come to sell anything."

There followed hard days for dear nurse. Frustrations! In Lisuland eggs usually abounded and chickens were the easiest meat to get. But two months in the year these two articles are scarce—August and September—and those were the months in which I took sick! To shorten the story, I lived, but with nourishing food so scarce it was decided to carry me out to Paoshan City. So, right in line with Mr. Fraser's prophecy that I would not be able to stand mountain rigors, ten months after arrival I was carried out again! Several months of rest and good food restored me, and Mr. Fraser gave permission for me to return to Oak Flat for Christmas.

Orders were that John build a better and healthier house, then we were to go on furlough. That gave us three more happy months at Oak Flat among the dear Lisu and with Job. I have always felt I owed my life to Job, as well as to Nurse Kathleen.

But why was this frustration of sickness allowed? One cannot always discern the reason for these things, but two are plain to us. (1) We learned that when one member of the party was thrusting out into Satan's territory, it was also necessary to put a prayer guard over those who stayed at home. We were all praying for John and his party as they pressed into the demon-plagued territory of Goomoo. Those prayers cleared the party's way (they were much blessed there) so Satan, in furious spite, struck at the unprotected home base. Both those who go down to battle and those who stay by the stuff need prayer-coverage. We have never forgotten this lesson.

(2) We learned that spirit and body cannot be divided. It is essential that one keep clean and yielded in the spirit, but the body's needs also must be cared for. That means bother. It means time spent on a garden, fruit trees, and perhaps a hen coop. We should not have been so totally unprepared for a hunger season. If the Cookes, our seniors, had been able to live with us and coach us, it would not have happened. But workers were at a premium, as I have shown, so we had to blindly pioneer our way.

We left for furlough in March, 1936. This book with subject matter, *platforms*—struggles of the soul—must necessarily pass over whole stretches of sunny, happy experiences. On this furlough we enjoyed comradeship in the things of the kingdom so full of joy, laughter, and fellowship with Himself that we turn to them over and over again in our memories with never-ceasing delight. This furlough also introduced us to the inheritance of saints which each had gained in marrying the other. My Christian friends were on the West Coast and John's were in Pennsylvania. Neither of us knew much about the other's friends, and on this furlough we met for the first time. Of my parents, only my father was alive. We went to see him before traveling to Pennsylvania and again at the end of furlough.

Our ticket to China was purchased and we were packed, ready to go on a Japanese boat sailing on Saturday at noon. Our farewell service was held in the China Inland Mission in Vancouver, B.C. We said good-by to our friends and returned to Father's house for our last night's sleep in the homeland. Almost as soon as we entered the door the telephone rang. It was Mr. Wilcox, our CIM secretary who had just farewelled us!

"There has come a telegram," he said, "from Dr. Glover [our home director]. He says that since war has broken out between Japan and China, all sailings must be delayed."

"Then we do not go tomorrow?" said John.

"Looks like it," was the sad answer. "Miss ——— is already on the boat! She got on at Seattle. Guess I'll have to ask her to get off when it stops here tomorrow. Too bad."

"Well, thank you, Mr. Wilcox," said John. He put the phone down and came in to face our amazed and incredulous group. Friends were with us at the moment.

"Well, we do not go, Belle, dear," said John quietly.

"Why not?" I was not in a mood to accept another frustration!

"War has broken out between Japan and China. The Mission is canceling all passages until the situation can be newly assessed."

"But the fighting is in the north in Manchuria, and we are going to the far south to Yunnan! There is no need to hold up either the Jack Graham family or us!" I argued.

"Now, Belle, don't try to run the Mission! We must just submit and do it happily," said John, who did not like it when his wife produced a disconcerting independence or when he thought she was trying to take the lead!

But here is where my experience of obstacles on the path of God's will stood me in good stead. John had encountered no obstacles in going to China; his path had been wonderfully clear.

"All obstacles are not from the Lord," I argued in alarm at his seeming passivity. "Dr. Glover gave a blanket order which is good for most of the cases. He has forgotten perhaps that two of the several families due to sail would be going south where there is not the least danger and won't be for a long time. Moreover, he probably does not know that there is a small inter-mission school for missionaries' children about to open in Kunming. He is thinking we need to take Kathryn to Chefoo, which is in the danger zone. If he knew there was a possibility of putting our children in school in the south, it would change the whole picture."

By this time our friends were taking their leave. They had promised to drive us to the dock the next morning and said that the promise would still hold good if we needed them. We said good-by and then turned to talk it out alone.

"Phone Mr. Wilcox and ask him, if you are in doubt," I suggested anxiously.

"Well, we will ask *the Lord* first," said my husband, firmly retaining his office is head of the house! "We have not had our evening devotions yet," and he reached for the Bible. We were following a certain course of reading so he opened where the bookmark lay. Then he looked up at me, his eyes twinkling, "Guess you win, Belle! Do you remember where our reading for tonight comes?"

"No."

"Psalm 91." We both exclaimed, "Wonderful. Praise His name!"

Then John read all those words of promise for times of danger, beginning: "He that dwelleth in the secret place of the most High shall abide under the shadow of the Almighty"—and ending—"and show him my salvation." When we had prayed, John got up, went to the telephone and called Mr. Wilcox. After explaining our thoughts, he was overjoyed when Mr. Wilcox answered, "I have been thinking the very same thing. I was just about to call you. I'll wire Dr. Glover immediately." It was then midnight, so we all went to bed.

But you can imagine we were up early, ears strained for the telephone. We were living at North Vancouver and it would take a good hour to motor around by the bridge to the ocean liner's dock. But it was nine o'clock before the answer came: I APPROVE. GLOVER. Oh, what jubilation! Everything was packed and ready to go, so into Betty's and George's car we piled and off we sped.

Frustrations. Those that are from the Devil we

must refuse in Christ's name. Mr. Fraser taught us to pray, "If this obstacle is from Thee, I accept it. If it is from the Devil, I refuse it and all his works in Christ's name."

My diary tells me we sailed on August 31, 1937, with Jack and Ella Graham and their two children, on the *Hikawa Maru*. This ship could not go farther than Japan but we were assured it would be possible to transship there for Hong Kong.

We had some adventures in Japan, but my next "platform" occurred on September 9, when our boat pulled into Hong Kong. I was thrilled and happy over the prospect of having Little Daughter in school at Kunming. John's sister, Kathryn Kuhn Harrison, and her husband were in missionary work in that big city, so our girlie could stay with her uncle and aunt—so I told myself. Imagine the shock, then, to find a telegram awaiting us at Hong Kong: "Send Kathryn to Chefoo with Grace Liddell." It appeared that Miss Liddell, one of our Yunnan workers, was going to Chefoo to help on the teaching staff. A safe boat had been procured, and Mission Headquarters thought it a golden opportunity to get Kathryn into our China Inland Mission School. It was, of course, much better equipped and staffed in every way than the little Kunming school. But I was totally unprepared to give up my girlie so soon.

I knew that, in one sense, it was giving her up for life. Although our Mission planned that children join their parents when possible for holiday times, one never again could watch them grow from day to day. The parting was excruciating for me, and for hours afterward I could not sit, lie down or do anything but grieve. I pored over all I would miss in putting her to bed at night, her sweet childish ways, the likelihood she would forget me to some extent—none of the poignant details did I miss. The consequence was that I was fearfully broken up. My dear patient husband walked the streets with me at night until I was so physically exhausted that I could lie down and fall into oblivion.

Our boat out of Hong Kong to Haiphong was delayed, and so there was time to spare. I remember going to a Bible class when the subject was "Praise." The teacher stood at the doorway shaking hands with us at the close. As she took my hand she looked at me very significantly and said, "The *sacrifice* of praise" (Heb. 13:15). My inward reaction was, "But you have no children!" It was true; she and her husband were childless. Nevertheless, she had planted a truth from the Word in my heart which I have never forgotten. There are times when it is sacrifice to praise Him, in the human sense. (In the light of Calvary nothing we can offer should be called sacrifice.) But there are so few things we *can* offer Him, this should be considered a privilege.

We took a boat to Haiphong and then through French Indo-China by train into Yunnan. It was during the long hours of sitting in the train that the Lord spoke to me. He said something like this: "Well, dear, you have *indulged your grief*. You have gone over your loss minutely and by detail. The last time you would give her a bath, the last night to tuck her into bed, the last energetic bear hug from the impetuous little arms, the last sight of lovely childhood sprawled gracefully in sleep, and so on. And now I would counsel you. What good did it do you? Emotionally you are as worn and limp as a rag. It did not profit you physically. It did not help little Kathryn at all. It was a drag on your poor husband. Of what use was it to indulge your grief?

"Next time—for this is only the first parting of many times to come—let Me counsel you to gird up your loins and try to be a soldier. There are many small helps you can use, especially in the area of the mind. Refuse to let your mind dwell on your loss. It will not make you love her less. Deliberately think of something more helpful, or anything rather than your loss. I have given you a thing called common sense—summon that to your aid. Common sense will tell you to avoid all scenes which harrow the feelings. Singing or music, for instance. Deliberately plan your good-by so that emotion will be strained as little as possible. When you return home after the loved one has left, change the furniture of her room around so as not to stir up memories which cause useless grief. And so on."

"But, Lord," I argued, "wouldn't that make me hard? I do not want to lose the ability to feel."

"You will not," He promised. "In fact, it will go all the deeper when it is not allowed to evaporate in bursts of emotion. Sublimate your feelings; re-channel your attention toward helping someone else. Amy Carmichael says, '*Help lame dogs over stiles. There are lots of lame dogs who have stiles to face—stiles harder than yours.*'"

And so He taught me—bless His precious name! Never again did I allow myself to be so broken up over a grief. And I found that common sense *was* a good aid. Also my love and my concern for my children certainly have never become less.

That train trip is wonderfully scenic as it climbs the heights toward Kunming which is 6,000 feet above sea level, and the beauty of my dear Lord's handiwork coupled with His direct dealing with me in my heart was healing and quieting to me. I needed it, because at Kunming another blow awaited me—another frustration.

It had never entered my head that perhaps the Mission would not reassign us to Lisu work. The reader will have foreseen this long ago, but I certainly did not. Mr. Fraser had prophesied I could not stand the rough mountain life physically and after only ten months of it I had to be carried out sick. Moreover, it had taken nearly two months' time from two other workers—Nurse Davies and Miss Embery—who had had to go in and help me. It was perfectly natural that the Mission should decide against our return to the Lisu. But it had never entered my wildest imagination, and our relatives (Kathryn and Dave Harrison) seeing that, pitied me. "Whatever will Isobel do when she hears she is not to return to the Lisu?" they whispered to one another.

On September 27, my diary tells me, we were called in for an interview with Mr. Fraser. He told us gently that we would be temporarily stationed at Paoshan "with freedom to go to Lisuland on trips." My diary also records that on that occasion he frankly stated he wanted John as his assistant superintendent for West Yunnan. This was not disagreeable to my hubby. He still enjoyed Chinese work equally as much as Lisu, so it was quite a happy designation for him.

Not so for me. I had always felt like a square peg in a round hole in Chinese work—partly no doubt because I had had to be a pioneer evangelist which was never my forte. Bible teaching was where I felt at home, and *mothering*. Miss Frances Brooke (author of *My Goal Is God Himself,* and one of my spiritual counselors for years) used to say that she considered my chief gift was that of mothering the Lisu church. I believe she was right. But there had to be converts already born again or a little church already formed before one could *mother* the people or break the Word in its deeper meanings to them. I had both in Lisuland, converts and churches. In Paoshan the church numbered but a mere handful and Miss Winifred Embery was mothering them very capably. At the same time a situation was arising in the Lisu church at Oak Flat which gave me much anxiety. My mother wings were fluttering in alarm over the young. On the first of October I decided to have a special time of prayer for Oak Flat and also lay before the Lord the soreness of my heart at being shut out of Lisuland. I did not want to stand in the way of my husband's promotion, but my heart seemed tied to the Lisu Christians. I must get the victory over it. For some years it had been my habit to fast and pray one morning a month for my own spiritual needs, the church's needs, and world revival. (Miss Ruth Paxson had started me on this habit.) My diary records that while I was waiting before the Lord on this occasion, He unexpectedly gave me some verses in Zephaniah 3.

> In that day shalt thou not be ashamed . . . for then I will take away out of the midst of thee them that rejoice in . . . pride. . . . I will also leave in the midst of thee an afflicted and poor people, and they shall trust in the name of the Lord. . . . Sing, O daughter of Zion. . . . The Lord hath taken away thy judgments . . . the Lord, is in the midst of thee: thou shalt not see evil any more. . . . The Lord thy God in the midst of thee is mighty; he will save. . . . I will save her that halteth. . . . At that time

I will bring you again . . . when I turn back your captivity before your eyes.

The first part of what I have quoted applied exactly to the Oak Flat situation. And the latter part I felt was God's promise to take me back into Lisu work.

I cannot tell you the joy and victory that flooded me. There have been times when the Word on which I was caused to hope was not *clearly* from Him. It might have been the product of wishful thinking. "Lord, keep back thy servant from presumptuous sins." On such occasions I would say, "I *think* the Lord wants me to do thus and so." But this promise was clear. There is a difference. He has promised that His sheep shall know His voice, and they do. I knew that morning that God had promised to clear up the situation at Oak Flat and to take us back into the Lisu work. *I knew,* and never doubted. So the garment of praise and singing was mine although I told no one, not even my husband. The Lord expects us to keep His secrets until His time comes to reveal them. Friends marveled at my happiness as we packed to go to Paoshan. They did not know the secret consolations of my dear Lord. This too is a part of the platform of frustrations—the end is that we may know Him and the power of His resurrection.

There was no Burma Road in those days—one traveled overland stage by stage. So it was October 27 when we arrived in Paoshan. My diary records: "Our two soldier escorts accepted Christ." Miss Embery and the Chinese church leaders came out to greet us and gave us a wonderful reception. We were there just a little more than a month when a letter came from Mr. Fraser saying he must ask us to make a trip to Oak Flat! The situation had become acute and, if the church was to be saved from a split, some missionary able to speak the language must go in immediately. He would love to have gone himself but he was too far away and tied up with other duties. We were also to act as escort to a new Lisu missionary, Victor Christianson, who was to stay at Oak Flat and learn the language. Mr. Fraser hastened to add: "Remember, this is not a permanent designation. You do not need to move all your things in. But you will need enough to set up housekeeping for a few months. It would be good for Victor to have the comfort of experienced seniors for a little while."

When I heard that, I slipped away to our bedroom and carefully closed the door. I did not want to shock my dear husband by my "unseemly levity." But when privacy was well secured, I danced with joy. "Temporary designation!" I gloated gaily. "So says you, my dearly beloved Super. So says you!"

He was indeed dearly beloved. He lived on the same high plane as Amy Carmichael and his godly life coupled with brainy leadership never ceased to inspire us. But he did not know of the Lord's promise to me to send me back to the Lisu.

"So says you," I continued, "but not so says the Lord!" Then, remembering what I owed to that dear Master, I dropped on my knees in worship. Really deep worship is wordless—words are too shallow to carry the weight of the heart's adoration. How wondrously He had wrought! He had promised to take me back to Lisuland—just between Him and me—and here, less than two months after arrival in Paoshan, we were on our way into Lisuland! December

13 we climbed the hill to the west of the city and set our faces toward the Salween!

Officially it was a temporary designation. We found the church much confused over law and grace and we felt that a longer period of Bible study with church leaders was needed. We suggested that the three months of the rainy season should be given to teaching. Mr. Fraser was very enthusiastic about the idea and so began our first Rainy Season Bible School (RSBS for short). It was a most blessed time—thrilling proof that this was what the Lisu church needed.

Then on September 30, 1938, as we were all packed to take a long trip into Burma to the famous Goomoo church, runners came with shattering news—*Mr. Fraser was dead*. He had contracted malignant cerebral malaria and never recovered consciousness. Our superintendent had gone Home to God. Personally I have never ceased to miss him. Nearly eighteen years have passed, but at crises of decision I still often think, "What would Mr. Fraser do?"

But to continue my story. With our superintendent gone, all missionaries remained at the station where they were, so the Kuhn family just continued on in Lisuland! Mr. Gladstone Porteous became superintendent for the province, but as Yunnan was such a large field he never once got west to visit us. At length, in 1940 it was decided to divide the province into east and west, and John Kuhn was made acting assistant superintendent of the west. This meant he was supervisor of Chinese as well as tribal work. From time to time a question arose as to the Kuhn family moving out to Paoshan where John would be near the telegraph office, so the matter of "temporary designation" hung over our heads for years.

After one of these times of acute question in the matter, I was passing by a group of Lisu church leaders who were talking together, when a remark dropped into my hearing. "We would never have had Ma-pa," one deacon was saying earnestly, "if Ma-ma had not loved us so dearly." It was a remark of shrewd perspicuity, and I pondered it as I walked on. I think he was correct. And then my mind glanced back many years to that conference in 1924 at The Firs, when Mr. Fraser had poured out his heart about the Lisu tribe, inwardly hoping for one of two brilliant young men who were present. He got neither, only a girl. Of what use was a girl? In God's unfathomable ways, she was to be the one who brought the needed man into the Lisu work. *Frustrations*—have much to do in conforming us into His image. Yes, suffering, but also His sweet consoling fellowship in that suffering. It reveals to us the power of His resurrection, and when He arranges a release for us that no mortal could manipulate—*we come to know Him.*

> Rock of my heart and my fortress tower
>   Dear are Thy thoughts to me.
> Like the unfolding of leaf or flower
>   Opening silently.
> And on the edge of these Thy ways
>   Standing in awe as heretofore,
> Thee do I worship, Thee do I praise
>   And adore!
>
> —A.C.

CHAPTER SIX

EXTINGUISHED CANDLEFLAMES

The sun went down in clouds,
The moon was darkened by a misty doubt,
The stars of heaven were dimmed by earthly fears
And all my little candleflames burned out.
But while I sat in shadow, wrapped in night
The face of Christ made all the darkness light.
—ANNIE JOHNSON FLINT

THE YEAR OF 1942 always stands out in my memory as my own personal experience of "the horror of great darkness." Life had been swinging along in great joy. Despite the ever-present physical trials of primitive living, the growth of the work and the delightful friendships it developed for us were sunny experiences. But with the year 1942 life turned a sharp corner. On the surface it was flung from pillar to post, emptied from vessel to vessel. But those were only what Bishop Moule calls "the outward woes of our inward pilgrimage." Inwardly I was set for a much-needed crucifixion of the flesh. But to see the picture properly, the outward woes must come first.

The Sino-Japanese war had been going on all these years, but we in the South had felt it only as a distant warning bell. But in 1941 the Japanese entered Burma and before the world's startled gaze they strode through that small land as with seven-league boots. We were working the mountains of The Hump, right on the China-Burma border north of the Burma Road. At the beginning of 1942 we were utterly unconscious that the Japanese would soon be within sight and sound! Generalissimo Chiang had lost province after province to them until in 1942 he had only three left—Yunnan, Kweichow, and Szechwan. Of these three, our province of Yunnan, with its Burma Road and airlift over The Hump, provided his only route of supplies. If the Japanese got Yunnan, all of China would be theirs.

Now as to my inward pilgrimage, there was an area of my life which the Lord had long needed to discipline. It was the area of the affections. I had always considered that this was one of my strong points!—a deeply affectionate nature. But the very intensity of such love has a danger—the danger of selfish possessiveness. Intense affection wants to hold on to the loved one and is unconsciously very monopolizing. Since God taught me this truth I have seen it many times in life. Such a pure love as mother love, if it becomes too possessive can blight the life of the child. "And they that are Christ's have crucified the flesh with the affections and lusts" (Gal. 5:24). I believe it is Conybeare who interprets *lust* as "a strong desire," so we may read that verse: "They that are Christ's have crucified the flesh with the affections and strong desires." I knew this truth before I came to China, but it was mere head knowledge. I did not know how to recognize it in my own life, let alone know how to deal with it. The time had come when I must learn. So in 1942 there began a systematic stripping away from me of all whom I loved.

First, my husband was called to a conference of superintendents in Chungking, and from then on events came in such a whirl that we were separated most of the year. Next, the Chefoo school, where Kathryn stayed, was captured by the Japanese, and my little girlie was wrapped in silence. Just now and again did a little childish note slip through to us, proof that she was alive and well. Before that, there had been a letter from her every week. Third, Mary Zimmerman, who acted as our home secretary, duplicating our circulars and forwarding to us news of and from our friends, fell silent. Her precious mother was taken Home to be with the Lord, and this sorrow was followed by a trial so disrupting that Mary just could not keep up her usual correspondence for about a year. Husband, child, friends, and then—my right hand in the Lisu work left us. It was for a very happy reason—our boy Lucius got married that year and had to set up his own home across the river. But nevertheless the very comfortable prop he had always been to me was missing. He alone had understood how much it meant to me to have a little corner where I could be private, when I had to live in a Lisu home for one or two weeks in order to hold a short Bible conference. To the Lisu mind, to be left alone is an affliction! They all sleep in the one room, two in a bed, and are gregarious by training. They would never dream of so ill-treating a guest as to give her a room to herself! Lucius did not sympathize with this queer desire of mine either, but he had learned that it meant a lot to me, and so when we traveled, in a nice way he would explain to our hostess Mama's queer liking for privacy. With a merry word here and there, he would himself rig up a screen

for me (if a room could not be obtained) behind
which I could retire to wash and sleep. No other
Lisu ever took such care of me. Of course, when I
traveled with John, he did that. But now I felt
stripped of every comfort indeed.

I was not so stupid but that I saw the stripping
was systematic and thorough — husband, child,
friends, and then my right hand in the work. I knew
it must be the Lord trying to teach me something,
but I was too lonely and heartbroken to submit.
"Lord, I was *made* to love and be loved. How can
I live without someone that is mine, *very specially
mine* above the rest around me? I'd rather be dead!"
So moaned the flesh as it was being set for the crucifixion of its inordinate affections. And with these
inner desolations the outer being was flung far
and wide as I am about to relate.

The year began happily enough. In February we
held our first Bible school for girls, with a success
that astonished the Lisu church, which had always
held that women could not learn! It was a triumph
and became a yearly event.

Then in March I developed acute toothache. I
tried to pacify it with medicines but did not suc-
ceed, for it was the Lord Himself beginning to spill
me out of my nest. The nearest competent dentist
was in Kunming, at the other end of the province!
In the old days it would have meant a thirty-day
journey, but now with the Burma Road open, it
could be done in about two weeks. Even so, it would
require two weeks to return, so I would be gone a
month or more! It was kindly veiled from me that
it would be *six months* before I saw Lisuland again!
The pain soon settled my hesitation, however—I
could not do any work until that ripping ache

stopped—so I called for porters to carry my things and escort me out to Paoshan. John was at the conference for superintendents in faraway Chungking. I could meet him at Kunming and we would return together—it planned itself very easily in my mind.

As I was about to leave Oak Flat I received a pleasant surprise—Lucius appeared, announcing he was going to escort me out, leading my mule for me over those precipitous and dangerous mountain roads, as had been his old familiar custom. He was building his new home (for him and Mary) and Paoshan was the best place to buy good nails. He would combine his personal business with the fun of escorting me again. To me, this was really a gift from the Lord, as Lucius was a delightful chatterbox, and his witty running-gossip of church and village life caused the long hours in the saddle to pass quickly. It was also a pleasant source of information of Lisu thinking and customs. I learned much from those hours in the saddle listening to Lucius talk. Besides this, he was a past master at making Ma-ma comfortable when we camped out at night. We had four-and-a-half days' journey to go. It used to be six, but the Burma Road had cut it short by that much. March 18 we started out, so says my diary, traveling about thirty miles and camping out at night in a big airy loft over a large horse stable! March is the beginning of spring, very often, in Lisuland. The old winter brown of the mountains is flecked with the light green of bursting buds. The pale pink of wild peach trees often dots itself against that bright green and old brown, and the delicate perfume of white rhododendron makes you catch your breath with joy and hunt for more of it. Distant mountain peaks are still snow-capped and

dazzling in the golden spring sunshine and the dear
cuckoo bird arrives to tell the Lisu to: "Plant corn!
Plant corn!"

Boy (as John and I usually called Lucius) chat-
tered happily about his plans and Mary's, and my
diary records that while we journeyed I translated
and taught him the chorus, "I'm Feasting on the Living Bread." He loved it and by the end of the trip
had it written down and ready to teach it to the
dear brothers and sisters at Olives on his return.
We caught a truck at the motor road and so got into
Paoshan by Saturday, March 21.

I had been dreading the Burma Road trip. There
was no regular bus service to the capital city (Kunming) and the only way was to go by a Chinese
merchant truck. Chinese drivers, looking for money,
regularly overloaded their trucks with merchandise,
and passengers were piled on top of that! You had
to climb up on top of all the boxes, bundles, and
bales and perch there, holding on as best you could.
Often I had seen such trucks with the top actually
swaying, as the driver, to save gas and so filch a
few pennies for himself, coasted down hairpin curves
with precipitous drops at the edge of the road.
And every now and again you came across the wreck
of a truck which had gone over, so you knew your
fears were not just imagination! The very thought
of Burma Road travel in those days still makes one
shudder. But the Lord had an unexpected kindness
waiting for me. (Note this: because 1942 was the
year when He had to give me a much-needed crucifixion experience, yet if you watch closely you will
see He was extra kind whenever it was possible.)
I was told that two of the Generalissimo's airmen
of the Flying Tigers were driving in a private car

to Kunming and would take me along with them. No Chinese truck-travel, but good American drivers! Wasn't that a kindness? My diary notes casually, "Rangoon has fallen"—to the Japanese.

We were to leave at half-past five in the morning, so I arose about four o'clock in order to have a quiet time with the Lord first. I had been up early so many mornings and traveling till dark, that I debated whether or not to skip my quiet time that day and get a little more sleep. But the habit of *God first,* formed in Moody days, stood me in good stead now. Whatever would I have done in the days ahead if I had missed that particular quiet time? For God had something particular to say to me. Yet when I lit my lamp at that early hour and turned my sleepy eyes on the portion for the day (Gen. 28) I had the feeling, "Oh, just the story of Jacob's ladder. Couldn't be anything special in that." Is it the lazy flesh or the Devil that puts such thoughts into our heads? I turned my sluggishness over to the Lord in prayer first, and then as I read that old story so familiar from childhood, verse 15 sprang out of the page as if I had never read it before. "*And behold I am with thee, and will keep thee in all places whither thou goest.*" The Lord's voice came clear and unmistakable: "This is My promise to you for the journey ahead." I thought He meant just that I dreaded Burma Road travel and I was grateful. So when Lucius came up to rope my bedding for me I told him I had received a verse from the Lord and roughly translated it. His face lit up and he beamed at me: "Praise the Lord! '*And will bring thee again into this land*'—He's going to bring you back again!" I stared at him. Bring me back? Why, of course I intended to come back!

Lucius must have missed the point. But, oh, how I had to thank the Lord later that it was Lucius who *got the point*—it was I who nearly missed it!

So I started out on the Burma Road trip with those two American air pilots. You will remember that the Flying Tigers were Madame Chiang's special proteges. They were tough but brave, daring men. They were not at all thrilled to have this drab-looking, uninteresting missionary woman tagging along with them, but were considerate and kind, as American soldiers usually are. Just once were we all really embarrassed. At Yunnanyi there was an A-V-G Hostel so the men put up there and got a cell for me. There was a lock on the door (Chinese inns seldom possessed such) and I locked it, fortunately. For about two o'clock in the morning a Flying Tiger arrived drunk. First thing I knew I was awakened by my door being shaken and pounded upon till I feared it must fly into bits. At the same time a drunken voice yelled, "Woman! Open zish door! I want to see zish woman!" A growl from a nearby cell proved that someone else was awake too, which comforted me. But it did not squelch the drunken ardor. "I don't care if she *is* a mishnary woman," he yelled back, "I want to see zish woman. Woman! Open zish door," and again that object was shaken till I quaked and prayed. Curses filled the air as the growler next door saw he would have to get out of bed to rescue me. Then followed a brief struggle interspersed with yells about the "mishnary woman," then finally the drunk was hauled off and shut up somewhere. The Flying Tigers were very nice to me until I tried to speak of Christ; then they became hard. They were tough and wanted to remain tough. Yet they were so kind too.

We were four days on the trip, and the fourth day the car broke down and there we were, miles from anywhere or any help—stranded. The American boys could not speak Chinese, so their idea was to wait in the middle of the road and hold up with a gun the first truck they saw, and compel help or transportation. They were disgusted with the Burma Road and its drivers. I begged them not to use guns and offered to interpret (hoping the Chinese language which I had not used for six years would come back to me). After an hour or so of uncomfortable experiences, a white man in a jeep appeared and offered to pick us up. He did not have room for all our baggage, so I had to leave my bedding roll locked in the back of the abandoned car. The Flying Tigers (thinking they were still in America?) meant to come back and get the car and luggage, but of course when they arrived, it had been plundered, so I lost my bedding roll and the clothing which was wrapped in it.

But I looked forward to the warm, hearty welcome Kay and Dave always gave us, for of course I planned to stay with my sister-in-law, although the China Inland Mission had a guest house in the capital city. Lonely and feeling ill, I pushed through the gate into the garden expecting to hear that pleasant yell of welcome as soon as someone spied me. But all was silent. Questioning, I went into the house and called. My voice echoed dismally, but no answer. From the back of the house came a patter of small feet and soon a rosy-cheeked Chinese maiden appeared. "Oh, *Yang-si-muh!*" she gave me my Chinese name, but spoke in English to me. "The Harrison family are all away in the country for meetings! But come in, I will take care of you." It was

Eva, who had been left in charge of the house. Eva was the oldest daughter of a Chinese pastor who had a large family. She wanted an education, so had come into the Harrison family to help with housework or cooking while she went to high school. She was a little thing in stature and looked only fifteen years whereas in reality she was twenty-one years old. People always thought Eva was a child, but she really was a very capable young woman, as I was to learn.

Eva was delighted to have company. She had now graduated from high school, which gave her a social status so that she was above the servant class, and it was quite proper to treat her as a companion. My Chinese was so rusty that I was pleased to hear her talk English, and she, on her part, was perfectly thrilled to get all these English conversation lessons free! So English was our medium by mutual consent. She soon had me in the Harrisons' own bedroom, and made me a tasty supper, for dark had fallen before we reached Kunming. It was March 27, 1942. I had made it in nine days from Oak Flat— very good time.

Now all those traveling days my tooth had not ached. Please notice that little kindness of the dear Lord. But I was feeling ill, looked ill, and had dizzy spells. The doctors had quite a time finding out what was wrong with me, but I will explain now so you will understand. A tooth which held a bridge had become abscessed. As the tooth was dead it did not ache—that is why the poison was so hard to discover. I had pains in my head, sometimes in my face, but never in that particular tooth. Yet the poison was going through my system and I really was ill. By the time the trouble was diagnosed and the tooth pulled, gangrene had set in. Our capable dentist said if I had come to her twenty-four hours later my life could not have been saved! It was more than two weeks after I arrived in Kunming that the tooth was discovered and all that time I was getting weaker and weaker. Alone in the house except for Eva, I was too ill to study or do much but lie in bed—and with plenty of time to brood over my loneliness!

All this time little Eva was a jewel. She would bake the nicest cookies and things to tempt my appetite, and in between meals she would sit beside my bed and chatter in English! It took my mind off myself so I encouraged her, and drew her on by questions about her life, studies, friends, and so on. As she answered I began to get a picture of an unselfish, hard-working young life that amazed me. She was quite unconscious of what she was revealing, for she had worked so hard that she never had time for self-consciousness. She was a Christian and the soul of honor. Meticulously careful about honesty, she leaned over backward to escape the slightest suspicion that she was misusing things that were accessible to her. For instance—the Harrison food cupboard. Every Chinese cook I had ever met helped herself freely to lard, sugar, and such things, not to speak of leftovers. But Eva never touched a thing for herself. I gave her money to buy my food and had not much appetite. To my dismay leftovers were carefully stored for me. She was one of those souls, rare in any nation, whom money does not tempt. She almost wept with chagrin when I offered her a little gift for her loving care of me. And she was that way all the years I knew her. I have met few like her in any land. Yet with her freedom from the greed of money, she was a most wonderful bargainer! She was of Szechwan extraction, and they are noted for their ability in that line. Eva could get more out of a dollar than anyone who ever helped me.

In addition to her honesty and industry, Eva was pure. Of course she was a daughter of Christians and had spent many years in a missionary's home, but that has been true of others who had not her love for purity. I have mixed with young people in these heathen lands, and even if their conversation was purged of the usual filthy joke of heathendom, it seldom reached the plane where a coarse or slightly shady story did not provoke a laugh. I have often been grieved and disappointed at this lack of sensitiveness to the beauty of holiness. But Eva was as chaste as anyone I ever met. One of the stories she prattled to me during those days related to a short train trip she had had alone—returning from the village to which the Harrisons had gone. "We were late getting in and dark had fallen. The train was so crowded and unpleasant that I found a spot all by myself on top of the baggage in the luggage car, but warm and cozy because it was next the engine. I was enjoying myself there when a man crawled up toward me. 'Sister, let's play together,' he said with an unclean smirk on his evil face.

"'You stay where you are!' I cried out. 'If you come one foot closer I will throw myself down under these train wheels!' He saw I meant it and with a curse he backed away. As soon as he was gone I slid down and went back into the crowded car. The conductor must have seen that man, for he came up to me, and pointing to the fellow said,

'Was that man troubling you?' The bad man gave
me such a wicked look I was terrified and replied,
'Oh, no.' He would have killed me in revenge if
I had told on him. People are found in Kunming
with knives in their backs all the time—no one knows
who has done it. But after that, the Harrisons would
never let me travel alone."

I thought this little story was very revealing, and
again cogitated on what a jewel this little Chinese
Christian girl was. I had seen Eva in the Harrison
household for years, but never realized what a fine
character was under that hard-working child-like
form.

As I had continued to get worse (nobody knowing it was just a tooth) the doctor wired for John
to fly to Kunming. The Chungking conference was
over, but he had been contemplating a trip to
Lashio—so reads my diary. He arrived Easter Day,
April 5. By this time the Harrisons had returned,
and loving care encircled me. But it was ten days
more before they discovered my illness came from
the tooth and pulled it, after which my strength returned rapidly.

During this time the Japanese were advancing
up Burma—the British retreating before them and
Americans evacuating. The Burmese began to flee
into Yunnan. We, at Kunming, had occasional air-
raid alarms. Then we heard that the Japanese had
taken Lashio, where John would have been if my
wire had not brought him to Kunming. Unknown
to us, the panic of the Burma Road had already
begun, and John, as superintendent, felt he should
go west to warn missionary families in isolated parts
to evacuate. None of them had radios and so might
not know of the danger. He planned to be gone

only a few days and then return to me. By then everyone was discussing the question—would Yunnan fall?

Just a week later, news came that the Japanese had bombed Paoshan without warning on a market day at noon. The carnage was terrible. My diary reports rumors that 15,000 were killed. Survivors stampeded onto the Burma Road in a panic to reach Kunming. Somewhere in the midst of it was John. Then on May 9 John himself arrived escorting Carl Harrison (who had been at school in Tali), Leita Partridge, Grace and Eric Cox and baby Miriam. These latter had barely escaped with their lives. As their truck was climbing the Salween Canyon the Japanese arrived on the opposite bank and opened fire! They abandoned the truck and the few possessions which they had hastily gathered together on hearing they must flee. What a story of wandering with an infant over wild mountainsides trying to find Paoshan! Then to arrive and see it in shambles! No missionary was killed, for those stationed there had all fled to our station of Oak Flat, thinking the Lisu mountains would be safe.

Four days later John left again for Tali to try to get other workers out. Then reports and rumors came piling in, one after the other. One such said the Japanese were advancing on us from three directions. We knew they had reached the Salween River in the west, for they had fired on the Coxes. Another report said a column was advancing up the Mekong River from the south of us. And another column of Japanese were said to be approaching us by the railroad from Indo-China to the east. The British and American consuls began to advise that women and children evacuate north to Chengtu. Everyone said Yunnan would fall.

Not yet a naturalized American, I came under the jurisdiction of the British consul, who did not hesitate to urge me to flee north. David Harrison was not home—he was out on a preaching trip in the country. In the Kunming Harrison household were only three women—Kathryn Harrison, a new worker (Evelyn Gibson), and myself. Four others of our missionaries, in the China Inland Mission guest house over the way, had decided to fly out to India. The consul had told us we might evacuate to India, or travel north to Chengtu with a Royal Air Force corps who were proceeding in army trucks. The British consul was irritated that I showed reluctance to leave. "Everybody is going to have to evacuate," he said, "and trucks are going to be at a premium. By staying on now you will be virtually taking the place on a truck that should be kept for the women and children even now fleeing toward us on the Burma Road. It is selfish to stay!" What should we do? If only John would return! But John was not my source of guidance. And the Lord was absolutely silent when we prayed for direction. Experience had taught me to stay where I was until He did speak.

But the RAF convoy was leaving early on May 17. May 16 we got word that the Japanese had *crossed* the Salween on the Burma Road. Still there was no guidance from the Lord. Stories of Japanese atrocities to women in Hong Kong and Burma poured in. The irate British consul sent me word *three times in that one day*, ordering me to go on the convoy the next morning. What should we do? We decided to go. We could take only a bedding

roll and one suitcase apiece. Of all one's goods—
what to pack in one suitcase? Dear little Eva went
crying around the house, helping us pack. If only
she could go too, she wept. "But since accommodation even for British women is difficult to find—how
could I ask them to make room for a Chinese girl?"
said perplexed sister Kathryn. Carlie, about six
years old, was with us too. Early the morning of
May 17, 1942, we three women, Carlie, and Eva arrived at the airfield where the convoy was. We
were praying for Eva's future—Kay wanted her
to go back to her own home. Then the Lord did a
kind thing. The RAF captain came around to check
on our identity, and saw Eva crying. Remember, she
looked like a child.

"What is she crying for?" he asked.

"She wants to come with us," answered Mr. Harrison desperately, "she doesn't want to be left behind."

"Oh, she's not very big," he said compassionately,
"let her get in—sure. That's O.K. What's her name?"
and the miracle was accomplished.

Eva had no bedding or clothes with her, but that
did not worry her. Sunshine followed showers. In
beside Carlie she hopped, and the convoy began to
move forward. Evelyn Gibson and I, with two RAF
men, were in one truck; Mrs. Harrison, Carlie, and
Eva in another; and I forget how many other trucks
were in the convoy. We had to sit and sleep in
the back of the truck. I remember that underneath
me was a spare tire and a typewriter (!), which in
turn were on top of ammunition boxes. I put Evelyn
next to the wall of the truck; I slept next to her,
and one of our men slept next to me. The trucks
must have been small, for that was all they would

hold. We ate RAF rations, and when we stopped for sleep the men had to take turns standing watch all night.

Seven days and six nights of such travel on the Burma Road! And plenty of time to think. Dust and rattle made conversation a burden. Out of sunny Yunnan into cloudy Kweichow. I had left my husband behind in Yunnan, and Evelyn had left her fiancé, Norman Charter. Sometimes I found her crying softly to herself, and that was how I felt too. But as I lay or sat there hour after hour, day after day, I was thinking. God had not told me to come—what would happen to me? Then I remembered Lucius' beaming face that last morning "Praise the Lord, Ma-ma," he had said. *"He says He is going to bring you back!"* Genesis 28:15 was becoming a worn place in my Bible. *"And behold, I am with thee, and will keep thee in all places whither thou goest, and will bring thee again into this land."*

"Well, Lord," I conversed with Him on the way, "maybe I'm out of Your will in this trip. You didn't tell me to come. But You let me be pushed into it. And You *did* give me Genesis 28:15 that morning. That I know. Now I claim the *all places* whither I go, and I claim the promise to bring me back. *This land* must mean Paoshan. So some day You are going to take me back to Paoshan. Of course I don't know when. But I have a feeling the Japanese won't get Yunnan after all. Oh, dear, why did I ever leave! And, oh, dear, my lonely heart—" and I twisted and squirmed with heartache.

As we passed through Pichieh, Kweichow, the convoy allowed us to stop and visit our missionaries there. Sister Welzel and Sister Hierle were so sweet to us but knew nothing of war conditions. They were carrying on as usual. We met some Miao tribesmen on the road and my heart twisted and tore itself anew at the memory of the Lisu and how far I was traveling from them!

Our RAF men were very good to us. A Scotsman named Davidson sat next to me most of the time, and he told me of the terrible carnage of Paoshan at its bombing. They had arrived (fleeing from Burma) at sunset of the day of the bombing and he said it was breaking day the next morning when they finally managed to get through—the destruction and carnage were so terrible. The RAF had been through all the Burma fighting, and their talk was gloomy—China would fall, for sure.

The afternoon of the sixth day when we pulled into Suyung, two CIM missionaries, Steven Knights and F. S. Bird, were waiting for us. They had had a telegram from our Headquarters in Chungking saying that their accommodations and those at Chengtu were full up—we were to get off the convoy at Luhsien, Szechwan, and stay with Mr. and Mrs. Arnold Lea until further notice. We arrived there the next afternoon at half-past four and were cordially welcomed by the Leas. Almost my first question was, "Has Yunnan fallen?"

"Why, no," said Mr. Lea in polite bewilderment. "War news seems rather good these last few days." It seems that Generalissimo Chiang had sent his crack regiment down a back road, chasing the Japanese back over the Salween River and holding them there. Yunnan was saved. And our flight had been perfectly needless.

Now I was two provinces away from Yunnan, with no possibility of getting back! Mr. Lea was very cordial, but one could see that he wondered why we had had to run *so far away!* There had never been any talk of Yunnan falling in their part of the world. I was heartsick. My life seemed one wreck of desolation, and the future black. What was happening to my little girl in Japanese hands? Well, the Leas had word that the school and children were being kindly cared for by their captors. Thank the Lord for that! A matter that made us all look sober was our extreme shortage of funds. Friends at home were giving generously, but the pegged exchange gave us only 50 per cent of the true market value. If only we could play the black market the China Inland Mission would be well off, but that was illegal and the Mission could not do it. So all of us were pinched financially. This made my return to Yunnan all the more hopeless. The RAF convoy had brought us free of charge, but if I returned I must pay my own way back—and suffer all those days and days on a Chinese truck on the Burma Road! My heart fainted at the thought.

The only thing to do, counseled Mr. Lea kindly, was to brush up on the Chinese language, settle down and help with the church work at Luhsien. So twice a week I went with the Bible woman to the Chinese prison. The Szechwanese dialect was very difficult for me to understand. Where the dialect I had learned pronounced a *j* sound, these people gave a *ts* sound, so that their sentences sounded full of hissings to me. Nevertheless they were needy souls, and the fellowship with Mrs. Ho was real. The prison was terrible—body lice crawling up and down the walls and everywhere. We had to change our clothes each time as soon as we returned from the place. But the poor women who were shut up there had to stay! Some accepted the Lord.

The weather too was terribly hot—100° F. (my diary reads).

Mrs. Harrison was not as discouraged as I. She would have to come this direction anyway, in a month or so, to put Carl into a new school which the China Inland Mission was opening in Kiating, Szechwan. So she had not lost any time really, and as Chinese was the language in which she worked, the adjustment of dialect was not difficult for her.

Eva, as usual, was making herself of value. She made the bread for all Mrs. Lea's big household (the Coxes and Miss Partridge had joined us now) and she was also sewing Carlie's new school outfit. She was a good little seamstress and could run a sewing machine better than I could. It was a big saving for Mrs. Harrison to get Carlie's things made so cheaply, yet so well.

Kay Harrison had received a letter from her husband which made us all feel bad. Dave felt that those rumors that Yunnan would fall had been the Devil's masterstroke. Not only had it scattered us to far Szechwan but other missionaries had flown out to India and left China entirely. His preaching band had heard the rumors also, got excited, and all had run home. "We were going to evangelize a part of the country that had been on my heart for years, and I had the best preaching band collected that ever I've had, and now—all dispersed. Refugees from the Burma Road are still piling in. Never have we had so many opportunities for service and—no missionaries! I hear that John is having a wonderful time in the west too. It is just heartbreaking that Satan has scored such a victory!"

You can imagine how this made me feel. Kathryn would have had to take Carlie to the new school at Kiating sometime anyway, so it was not such a great loss to her. But for me, I simply ate my heart out with grief. Even my hair went dead until someone said it looked like straw. My diary for June 4 records that Mr. Lea had a talk with me suggesting that maybe I could help in the new school at Kiating. This really flattened me. It showed that Mission leaders were trying to find a place for me in the province of Szechwan. But my husband was in Yunnan! And my dear Lisu—O Lord, what should I do?

Never had the Lord's presence left me. Frequently He gave me comforting Bible verses, assuring me of His love. "But I'm a human being, Lord," I wailed. "It's a human touch and love that I crave so! And not just anybody's—I want *my own*. *My own!*"

The next day came a letter from John telling of wonderful opportunities he was having. "I do so wish you were with me, dear," he wrote. He had joined Dr. Wesley Mei's Medical Unit. Cholera had broken out after that terrible Paoshan bombing and they were inoculating the refugees—hundreds of them. And hearing their stories too, of course. Hearts were bleeding and just ready for the Balm of Gilead. Then I began to question, "Lord, may I not go back?" I spoke to Mr. Lea about it. He was kind but looked a bit alarmed. "You were sent here by recommendation of the British consul. They are still fighting in Yunnan. I do not see how you could return without the consul's permission— and I'm sure he'd never give it just now. Besides, there are plenty of trucks still fleeing from Yunnan but very few returning to it. I do not know that you could get conveyance there."

But I was getting more and more desperate.

"*I will bring thee back into this land*"—Lord, You promised that! Now help me get back." The next day I wrote to Mr. J. R. Sinton, who was acting in the place of our general director those days. I told him I felt I should return to Yunnan and of the opportunities Dave and John wrote about. Then I had to wait for an answer. In the meantime another letter came from Dave Harrison saying he could see no reason why Isobel should not return! Still Mr. Lea was dubious about a woman going alone on a Chinese truck all that long way, and without consular permission! On June 13 Mr. Sinton's answer arrived. He was very nice, but advised my waiting until my husband invited me to return. That was enough for me. The next day was Sunday and I took the morning off for fasting and prayer. It was no small thing to act without consular authority; for I had decided it would be useless to apply for it. I must just slip back without telling him. But the main thing was the *Lord's* permission. I did not doubt that He had promised to take me back to Paoshan; the point was, *when?* Was it to be now? Or should I wait for two more weeks? I went out into a Chinese cemetery and there among the graves, undisturbed by spectators, poured out my heart to Him. I had four difficulties to lay before Him—the very first being an utter impossibility. Quite simply I did not have enough money for that long trip! Some gifts had come through, but our account had been very low. And I not only had the expense of getting to Yunnan, I still would have to cross almost the entire province before I reached Lisuland again! And the exchange was still impossibly low. So my requests were laid out this way.

1. Money to make the trip.

2. John's invitation—to satisfy Mr. Sinton. "It would be nice to have you here," might not be recognized as an invitation in Headquarters' eyes.

3. Trucks going to Yunnan. They were very few.

4. I dreaded going alone with Chinese men. A companion, Lord?

Within just a little more than twenty-four hours the Lord had answered all four.

Special gifts arrived in the mail.

A telegram from John arrived, urging me to join him.

Mr. Lea found a convoy of three merchant trucks going back to Kunming.

Eva asked to go with me!

The money was the biggest miracle of all. Years before, John had received a legacy. Learning that a certain young Bible student had not sufficient funds to finish her course, we had given her $100.00. She wrote us that if ever she was able, after graduation, she would repay us—but we merely laughed at that. We gave it as to the Lord and forgot about it. I had truly forgotten all about it. But the Monday after my prayer day, the mail brought two letters from this girl. These letters were written and posted *six months apart*, yet they arrived in the same mail. *And each letter contained $50.00 U. S.!* The marvel of it has never left me.

The gift of Eva was just as unbelievable. That previous Saturday morning as I passed through the laundry I saw Eva scrubbing some of Carlie's clothes and silently weeping. I did not know what had caused her tears and did not feel I should ask. But I did know that whatever the trouble was, her Lord could help her. So I put my arm around her

and whispered, "Tell the Lord about it, dear. He
can help you," and then went on my way.

When the money for my return trip arrived so
miraculously, of course I ran in to tell sister Kathryn. Eva, sewing in the corner, heard me say I had
money to take me back to Kunming! Now her tears,
unknown to me, had been because there was no
money *for her* to return! Shortly after I had gone
back to my own bedroom, sister Kathryn appeared
at my door.

"Eva says she would like to go back with you.
She says she will go and work for you in Lisuland
if you will take her. I have no money to pay her
return expenses, and I will not need her at Kiating
where I am going, so if you want her and can pay
her fare, why—take her!"

I was dumbfounded. I could not believe my ears.
To me Eva was a rare jewel of a helper whom
nobody would ever willingly relinquish. I was afraid
Kathryn might regret it, as soon as bank exchange
righted itself and finances did not pinch us. But
she said, "No, if you want Eva, take her."

I had been praying for a companion, but had
wildly imagined some other white lady might by
chance be going back. I had never once thought of
Eva. To tell the truth, we missionaries to the Lisu
did not approve of bringing Chinese helpers into
tribesland. They almost always considered themselves so much better than the Lisu, and were so
patronizing to them that it caused trouble. Little
Eva? I still wondered if I should promise to take
her to Lisuland. To Kunming, yes. Lisuland was a
little different. But Eva begged to go.

"I do not want your money," she said with tearful eyes. "I will serve you for instruction in Bible,

English, and music. I want to learn to play the organ. I do not eat much, and I have enough clothes at Kunming to last for several years. Please take me."

"Well, I will take you to Kunming," I said. "But there is Mr. Harrison to ask also. You have been a wonderful helper in their home. Maybe he will not be happy that his wife has offered you to us. If he is not happy, I will leave you at Kunming. In the meantime you can pray about it."

The very next day Mr. Lea got us our trucks. The one we were to ride was a brand-new one, and by paying the truck company a little extra, we obtained tickets for two seats in the cab beside the driver. That meant we would not have to perch on top of baggage, and we would not be exposed to rain or bad weather, for it was the rainy season.

We were introduced to our driver by the company manager, and he bowed, smiled, and was so pleasant that Mr. Lea commented on the fact. "These three trucks are going right through," said the manager. "They are not allowed to pick up yellow fish."

Yellow fish was the term used for a passenger picked up illicitly on the Burma Road by truck drivers. Their fares went into the driver's pocket instead of into the coffers of the company who owned the trucks. And the drivers charged what they thought they could get—it was a nefarious traffic.

We were to leave the next morning. I prayed on Sunday and we left on Wednesday—that is how fast the Lord worked for me.

However, we were no sooner out of sight of Lu-hsien City than our driver changed his manners toward us. All the smiles left and he became nasty. All along the country roads he stopped and picked up the forbidden yellow fish. At the main cities his truck company had inspection posts. Just before arriving at these, the truck stopped and all the yellow fish had to get off and walk through the city and beyond the inspection post to the farther side, where we picked them up again. Their baggage was cooly attributed to Eva and me, who, of course, had very little. Eva and I, having bona fide company tickets, were saved all this bother. While we were still in populous Szechwan and Kweichow our driver was not too uncivil, because twice we stayed overnight in towns where the China Inland Mission had missionaries living, and he saw that we had friends to whom we could have reported his ill-conduct. But once we began to go over the lonely mountain ranges into Yunnan, our driver showed his real colors. At one isolated spot, he stopped the truck, walked out in front of us and deliberately showed us he was an immoral man. Of course we refused to look, but Eva caught my hand in terror. "Don't be afraid, dear." I whispered, "the Lord is with us." And in my heart, "You promised, Lord! *Genesis* 28:15: '*I will keep thee in all places whither thou goest.*' This is one of the all places." But I now knew that we had an unclean as well as unprincipled man to deal with. I feared most for little Eva, and never let her out of my sight. The driver became nastier and nastier to me, snapping savagely at any chance to order us around.

When at length we pulled out of Kweichow, where the skies were overcast all the way, and crossed the boundary into Yunnan, the sun burst forth in a golden glory lighting up the green of beautiful mountaintops. "Now I know," I said to Eva, "why they named our province *South of the Clouds*. We are south of cloudy Kweichow." And in my heart was a burst of joy to be back again in the same province, at least, with John and the Lisu. But our worst trial lay ahead. From Kutsing we hoped to make Kunming in one day. But that morning as we gathered before the three trucks, it was raining. Some Chinese women appeared on the scene. Yellow fish? No—free passengers, friends of the drivers. To my astonishment my driver came up and said with a nasty look, "You are to get into truck number two. There is no room for her" (indicating Eva); "she can ride up in the back of my truck."

"I am very sorry," I replied politely but firmly, "but we cannot separate. And Miss Tseng must have a cab seat. We have paid for cab seats."

"Well, you can't have it!" he swore at me. "There aren't enough cab seats. These ladies" (his smirking girl friends) "are relatives high up in the company. They come first."

Then my indignation took fire.

"Look here," I said, speaking plainly (a deadly breach of Chinese etiquette), "we have paid extra for cab seats and we are going to have them and sit together. You have been taking on yellow fish. If you do not give us our seats I'll report you to your company!"

Then he really got furious. I knew he was swearing at us but his words spat out of his mouth so fast and his eyes glared and snapped so that I was lost in the torrent of Chinese language. Eva, however, understood. She began to cry, "Oh, *Yang-si-muh*, you don't know what he is saying! I don't mind standing in the rain! Let me go. He says he is going to throw us out on the lonely mountainside and leave us to the wild beasts. Oh, don't make any more fuss—I'll go!" Was there ever a blacker moment? No one in Kunming knew when we were to arrive, so our nonarrival would not alarm our friends there— they might wait a month without concern for us. Another foreboding fact was that I did not have consular authority to return, so how could consular protection be asked? But there is always One with us who is greater than the governments of this world. Again desperately in my heart I cried, "Lord, Your promise! *'I will keep—.'*"

I had not time to finish the verse before a hand plucked my sleeve from behind and a Chinese voice whispered hoarsely, "Get into my cab, quick—both of you!" We whirled around and sprang into the cab of the second truck. The driver shot into place behind the wheel, raced his motor, and off we sped, leaving my driver still swearing and trembling with rage. We were now in a much older truck, one that had broken down several times during the trip, but as we sped along into a good lead over the other trucks, our new driver turned to me and said quietly, "Lady, never do that again! Next time you travel the Burma Road, *you travel yellow fish.*" All day long we kept in the lead and out of sight of the other trucks. And all day I prayed that this old truck would not break down again. And it did not. Another Chinese woman was with us, so that Eva had to sit on my knee or partially so. But our driver was very courteous and drove us right up to the Harrisons' door. Luckily our baggage had been placed on his truck. We were safe. *"I will keep thee."* He had kept. He had never promised that we would not have trials.

Dave Harrison gave us a resounding welcome and

soon Eva was back in her old place making us tasty meals.

A letter from Mary Zimmerman was waiting for me.

This dear friend had formed the habit of writing us long, newsy letters, quoting from letters which spoke of our circulars, so that a letter from her was like a round-robin from everybody. I had so missed them: it was wonderful to be in touch again. Rain and more toothache and another visit to the dentist are recorded in my diary.

Before our flight to Szechwan, Kathryn had been teaching a Bible class attended by some twenty-seven university students. Dave had taught this class during our absence, but he wanted to make another trip to some needy country churches. Would I please delay going west about a half-month to teach these English classes for him until he could get back? There was really no hurry for me to return to Lisuland. The missionaries from Paoshan who had refugeed to Oak Flat would teach the Rainy Season Bible School by interpretation, so the Lisu were taken care of. It was these Chinese students at Kunming who might disperse if the classes were dropped.

As for Eva, Dave was quite pleased that she go with us to the Lisu. Since she had graduated from high school, Eva's mother had been angry at her doing servant's work in the Harrisons' home. Several times she had made it unpleasant for them, so Dave would be glad if Eva went with us. But for the next two weeks—would I stay?

It was clearly my duty. I have heard some say that the need is not the call. I do not understand that. An obvious need is a call in any branch of human life. The Good Samaritan did not need a special Bible verse miraculously shining upon him to indicate that it was God's will he help the poor fellow who had fallen among thieves. Where common sense clearly points out a duty, that is the voice of God. We do not need any other, provided a higher duty is not claiming us. For a mother to cast aside her own child in order to go and care for a neighbor's would not be God's will. She owes a higher duty to the human soul which she herself has brought into existence. Apart from that, the need is the call.

I did not want to stay in Kunming. I wanted to get to John as soon as possible. I was desperately longing for *one of my own* to put his arms around me and comfort me. But dearer than any human love is the Master's, and I could not grieve Him by disobedience. So I consented to stay, and Dave joyfully went on his trip.

The students' class began to grow. One day I was asked if I would not teach a second Bible class: the evening class was mainly evangelistic, but some of these university students were now Christians and wanted deeper teaching.

One tall young Manchurian, Jack W———, was especially eager. When the Japanese conquered Manchuria, Jack's school had evacuated and he with it. He had married in his early teens, and when he fled from Manchuria he had a little daughter two years old. As the Japanese advanced, his college fled before them until finally they had reached Kunming. During the first few years away from home Jack had corresponded with his wife, but for some years now he had received no word from her at all. He did not know if she and the little daughter were alive or dead.

At Kunming Jack had heard of Mrs. Harrison's English classes and had started to attend. Here he met the Saviour and gave his life wholeheartedly to Jesus Christ. Jack was really born again and hungry for a deeper life with the Lord. I believe it was he who asked me to begin a morning class for Christians, and I was delighted to do so. Evangelism was never my gift, but the opening of the Scripture feeds and blesses the teacher even more than it does the student. I loved to teach the Bible. By July 7 (my diary records) I was teaching three classes, and one young man had accepted Christ as his Saviour. But when Dave came back from his trip and could take over the classes. I felt released. Then the Lord worked for us. A Friends Ambulance Unit (English) was driving to Tali and they offered to take Eva and me with them. Oh, how grateful I was that we need not travel that stretch of the Burma Road on a Chinese truck! It was still the rainy season and we needed cover. We left Kunming on July 15.

Jack W——— came down to see us off, expressing deep thanks and saying he had been much helped. The FAU truck was delayed several hours but Jack waited all that long time with us to make sure we got off safely. I never could forget that kindness and we corresponded a bit from then on.

I would like to digress a moment to tell more of Jack. As soon as he was saved, he became burdened for his wife and her need to know the Saviour if she were still alive. He had not seen her for ten years then, and the ordinary Chinese would have laughed at the thought of loyalty to her under such circumstances. It was good Chinese custom for a man to have a concubine to travel around with him, while the legal wife was left at home. Jack was tall, good-looking and personable. He was not even sure that his wife was alive. Why be so finicky? The only reason was the command of His Lord and Master, Jesus Christ.

Seven more years of silence passed. Still Jack was clean and single. By that time he was an ordained Episcopalian clergyman and had friends who were willing to send him to America for further training. That was, to any Chinese, a tremendous temptation. Study in America was the acme of good fortune to a young Chinese of those days, and Jack was human enough to feel the pull of it. He wrote to me about it, asking prayer for guidance. "I would love to go to America," he said, "but somehow I canont get away from the burden of my wife and family. It is seventeen years since I saw them last. My little two-year-old girl will be a young woman of nineteen now. I feel I should try to go and find them. Please pray with me, Mrs. Kuhn, that the temptations of this world will not sway me but that I may do only the will of the Lord Jesus."

A few months later another letter dated from Peking. By this time the communists were in control of Manchuria. I do not have the original letter, but in substance it ran thus:

DEAR MRS. KUHN:

I decided to do the will of the Lord and go in search of my family. I resigned my position in Yunnan and came here hoping to get information as to how I might gain entrance to Manchuria. I found I could get a seat on a plane tomorrow, but it is a very dangerous procedure for a Christian to try to do this. I am afraid. Oh, pray for me that my faith may not fail!

I looked up the Christian family in this city whose address you gave me. They were very kind to me and asked me to supper. But, oh, Mrs. Kuhn, why is it that so few Christians ask to have prayer with me?

I fly in tomorrow. If it is possible, I will write to you from there. If you never hear from me again, you will know it was only because communication with you was not possible.

Then followed silence—for three long years. Then through a very roundabout way, sister Kathryn received a message. "I found my family. They have become Christians and the Lord has given us a little son." So ends one of the sweetest little idylls that I know of Christ's Round-Table Knights in China.

And now to retrace our thoughts back to July 17, 1942, and the Friends Ambulance Unit which was pulling into Tali with Eva and Ma-ma on board. (Since she was coming to Lisuland, I taught Eva to call me by the name which I loved most to hear from Lisu lips, *Ma-ma*.) I was longing to meet my husband. He had been writing to me from Tali, had approved my delay in order to set Dave free for country work, but looked forward to my joining him at Tali as soon as Dave returned. So I was all set to meet my dear husband whom I had not seen for more than two months. Imagine the shock I felt, on arrival in Tali, to be told that John had gone on to Paoshan with Dr. Mei and the Medical Unit! I was simply shattered. "You'll never have *anyone* to love you," mocked Satan, taking advantage of my self-pity. "God is a jealous God.

He doesn't want you to have anyone but Him to love you." It is very devastating to lend your ear to the Evil One. If only we could learn that he never tells the truth! Not the whole truth; a half-truth he tells, which is ever the worst of lies. God *was* loosening my hold on human love; He *was* nailing my affections to the cross. But not that my life should be without love and loved ones. Merely that the inordinate affections should become ordered. The human props on which I leaned so heavily were bound to give way sometime or other, just because they were human. And then when they gave way—how painfully I sprawled! If I could only learn to receive my loved ones, and yet not lean so heavily on them. Hold them, and yet not be so dependent on them! It was Love, and tender anxious Love, that was disciplining me. And I was learning, although with such agony.

Eva, for instance, was always watching to help me. But already I was alerted to the danger this could become. "Watch that she does not become indispensable to you," was the Lords' tender warning in my ear. "If you clutch her to your heart and she becomes as indispensable as these others, you will have all this pain to go through again, for human props will always fail, sometime or other. Lean more on Me, dear. I will never fail you nor forsake you." And so in loving Eva, there was now *harnessed affection*. Always I reminded myself to live in the light of the day when I must give her up to someone else.

But I was slow to learn. The day after arrival in Tali my diary reads: "At noon I got a letter from John. He is not coming back until August! I felt so heartbroken, Father, dear! But then I received a

letter from Girlie, *the first one in over seven months.*"
It was written before they were interned, but after
the Japanese had commandeered the school. Here
is her letter:

Chefoo, May 12

My dearest, darlingest, own Mummy and Daddy,

I'm afraid to say that you owe a lot to Auntie
Roxie [Mrs. J. O. Fraser] for again she invited me
out from Tuesday till Saturday. At breakfast she
used to always make me eat a lot, then because we
don't have bread ration there at breakfast as we do
at school but for supper we each had six pieces of
bread put on our plates, and then we all mixed pea-
nut butter and syrup together and put it on our
bread. Margaret never ate the whole of her ration
so the rest was given to me.

On Thursday they had all the second formers out
for supper—it started raining and we found out they
had all been for a picnic dinner. We played games
and in the end it cleared up and we went to the
Old Prep. While we were there we ran out of water
and had to get some from the McMurrays. The
next day the McMurrays invited us all out for the
day. Fortunately it was Dorothy's birthday but they
did not know. We had a lovely time. In the afternoon we watched Edith having a bath, then she
asked me to undress and bathe Betty, the older of
the two. She was very good until it came to taking
her out she just cried her heart out almost, she had
a little habit of holding her ears when she cries
but she just stood there shivering. It was the first
time I ever bathed a baby. In the afternoon Auntie
Roxie told them they had chosen the right day.

On Saturday Auntie Roxie invited Dorothy's form
for supper and again it turned out rainy but still
we went to the Old Prep and we had supper and
a game of hide-and-go-seek then we went home and

as soon as we got in, it poured so we were safe. Then because Catherine was staying until Monday, Fitz invited me up for the week end. On Sunday morning I woke up with a wart on my foot which is now plastered up.

With much love,
KATHRYN

This happy letter reminded me that the dear wife of our late superintendent would mother my girlie in internment camp, which she did. And all this time in Tali the Lord was working for me that I might not be tried above that which I was able to bear (I Cor. 10:13).

I inquired about Eva and myself proceeding to Paoshan, but found a new difficulty. Tali was the last civil post. All west of Tali was in the *military zone* now, for the Japanese were still within the province. They were on the west bank of the Salween River, and the Salween Canyon (Lisuland!) was now the front line of battle. No one could go west of Tali without a military pass. Even American soldiers were not allowed as far as the Salween! They chafed to get there but the Chinese were jealous of the front line and would not admit them. Paoshan was only one day's journey from the Salween. John had gone through because he was attached to Dr. Mei's Medical Unit *which was Chinese.* If American soldiers were not allowed at the Salween, how could I, *a woman,* ever get there? Please ponder that. Against it put God's Genesis 28:15—"*and will bring thee again into this land.*" Oh, how I clung to that, and how I claimed it in His presence! Ten days the Lord kept me praying and claiming that verse. Now watch how wondrously He worked.

John kept writing to me, urging that Eva and I join him in Paoshan. He seemed to forget that we could not leave Tali without a military pass. At length I decided to go to the residence of General Song (head in command of the Western Yunnan front) and ask for a pass to Paoshan for Eva and me. I shrank unspeakably from asking favors of these high-ranking Chinese. My best clothes I had left stored in Paoshan—they were stolen in the looting which took place after the bombing. Expecting to stay in Kunming only a few weeks I had not brought much with me, and some of what I brought was lost in the Flying Tigers' car which broke down. Missionary friends had given me some of what they could share, but I was painfully conscious of my shabby appearance. This did not help to give me poise. I got no farther than the outer gate of General Song's estate! His soldiers looked me up and down without much respect, kept me waiting a long time, and then sent me home without any pass! I learned later that they had not even sent in my application. This is what happened when I tried to move in my own strength. But see what happens when God moves!

That very evening an officer arrived at our China Inland Mission Compound "to inform Mrs. Kuhn that General Song had telephoned to Paoshan and requested that John Kuhn come to Tali—the general providing transportation!" The reason for this was not divulged at the time, but I was told to expect my husband soon.

The reason, unknown to me then, was this. Checked at the Salween Bridge on the Burma Road, the Japanese had gone north up the canyon, seeking another crossing. The tribes (heathen) in those parts had received and helped them. Suddenly China had awakened to the importance of possessing the friendship of these poor "earth-people" as they had for centuries termed the tribes. But in order to solicit their co-operation it was necessary to speak to the tribes and—who knew their language? The feudal lairds, of course. So these were summoned to Tali and their influence requisitioned. But it was very soon evident that they were utterly undependable— they would sell the tribes to the highest bidder. Was there no one else who spoke Lisu? Then it was that the Lord brought the American missionaries to the general's mind. Hence the phone call for John. He arrived at Tali August 4, and what a reunion it was!

That afternoon we went together to see General Song. I had a different reception this time! The officials at the gate bowed and scraped to us, and we were taken right into the beautiful mansion which was the home of the Songs. The general was very cordial to us and quickly summoned his charming wife, who spoke English well. It was then he told us frankly of his interview with the Salween feudal lairds. "Why, I found they were all opium sots!" he exclaimed. "They cared about nothing but opium. I couldn't use them, so I sent for you—will you help us solicit the friendship of the Lisu people?"

We told them we had already done so. We had told the Lisu that the Japanese would oppose their being Christians—that alone was sufficient. And it is significant to me that the Japanese won the west bank of the Salween up to the point where the Christian church became numerous. From there on they were held back, and conquered no more!

General Madame Song invited us to go with them

to Hsi Cheo the next day for an outing. Hsi Cheo was at the head of lovely Lake-of-the-Ear, where Central China University had refugeed. It was a beautiful day and we rode in the general's car with his family. (Their little boy was named Richard and the little girl Annabelle.) Dr. and Mrs. Logan Roots were with that university and entertained us to a delicious American lunch. The general had been invited to address the university student body, and we were ushered in as honored guests of his retinue! In his speech General Song exhorted the students to take the minority groups of their country upon their hearts and devote their lives to helping the mountain tribes. "Now," said he, "when China needs the friendship of the tribes on her border, she has to turn to Americans"—and here he indicated John and me with his hand—"in order to solicit their co-operation. Shame on us that there have not been some Chinese philanthropists to take an interest in these peoples!" But his harangue produced nothing more than assent that it would be a good thing. Most of these students were heathen, and it is only the constraining love of Christ that could sustain one through the physical hardships of life in the Salween gorge—that, or the mistaken passion of Communism. All the years I have been a tribal missionary I have never known anyone to go to the tribes merely to help them except these two classes—Christ's missionary and the Communist idealist.

General Song told us he would give us a military escort right to Oak Flat Village! And John was to be made adviser to the Nationalist guerrilla colonel in charge of the Pien Ma Pass district (which was our Oak Flat church area). We were to leave in a few days.

On our last night in Tali (so it was meant to be, but we were later delayed) the Songs invited us to a Chinese feast in their home. It was a sumptuous affair, and Madame even had a lace tablecloth spread for our benefit. (Chinese custom does not use table-cloths, as their tables are beautifully polished lac-quer.) I remember one dish appeared to be roast chicken—it was brought in with wings and legs prop-erly trussed.

"Have you seen this dish before?" asked Madame Song, who enjoyed my undisguised admiration of her cuisine. She took her chopsticks, stuck them into the breast-bone ridge of the chicken and with a flick of her finger the chicken fell open. It had been completely boned! How they ever maintained that perfect shape without any bones to hold it together is still a mystery to me!

Before the meal ended, General Song gave a com-mand and a smartly uniformed colonel was ushered in.

"I wish to introduce you to Colonel Hsie, who will be your escort to the Salween," announced the general. Then turning to the colonel he issued crisp orders that we were to be well taken care of. It was like a dream. Not only a military pass to a point which might at any moment become front line of battle, but an escort too—and all expenses paid! Only God could do that. "*And I will bring thee again into this land.*" But I yet had need to claim Genesis 28:15 once more, before getting there.

Dr. Roots had asked permission to ride with us as far as Paoshan, where Dr. Wesley Mei's Medical Unit was still working. We were given a brand-new truck for the trip. Eva and I sat in comfort in the cab, with the driver, while Dr. Roots, John, Colonel

Hsie, and the soldier escort rode in the open back.

The afternoon of the second day's travel we had come to some of the famous sharp curves of the Burma Road, with unguarded precipitous drops at the edge. I do not know anything about driving, but as we whirled around these hairpin turns and gaily struck big stones lying on the rough road I thought to myself, "Guess it is all right, but this looks to me like dangerous driving." I was just wondering about it, when we struck another large stone; there was a ripping and a pounding noise. The entrails of the engine semed to fall out—*bang! bang! bang!* Something underneath was dragging and bouncing, the brakes were broken and the wheels would not respond. The side of the road dropped away in a precipice. I heard John screaming, "Jump! Belle! Jump!" But where to? Outside of the cab door was the edge of the precipice! I just sat still and cried in my heart, "Lord, *You promised! 'I will keep thee in all places whither thou shalt come and I will bring thee again to this land'*—it's not Paoshan yet!" I was still quoting Genesis 28:15 when the driver somehow managed to turn the wheel in toward the steep rock bank of the mountainside and away from the dangerous edge. Then Eva and I opened the cab door and got out.

What a sight met our gaze! Soldiers were lying in the rough gravel road with heads gashed open, bloody and groaning. Dr. Roots, John, and Colonel Hsie had jumped running, of course; but the poor common Chinese soldiers, just off the farm and with no experience of trucks or modern machinery, had jumped straight. The next few minutes were busy ones: Irate Colonel Hsie was shouting orders to tie up the driver (it was a brand-new truck, you know); Dr. Roots was kneeling beside the wounded with his first-aid kit open. "Build a fire and boil some water for sterilizing," he called to us. A fire?—in the middle of the Burma Road? Unpractical me—I stood and gaped. It was little Eva who ran to the hillside to look for twigs, and it was she who got a fire going and boiled water in a surprisingly short time. I helped hold heads up while the gashes were bathed clean and the doctor bound them up. Straightening up to ease my back at one time, I looked over the edge of the precipice and gasped in astonishment to see, about a hundred feet down, the wreck of what once had been a truck! I called John's attention to it: "Hm," he grunted. "One has gone over here, sure enough. It's a miracle we didn't go too." Incidentally, we had a good chance to preach Christ to those poor soldiers of our escort.

Stranded on this lonely stretch of the Burma Road, six or seven miles from Wa Yao, the nearest village, we had nothing to eat, and darkness was approaching. Colonel Hsie was still flying around, making one of the soldiers climb a telephone pole. Soon I saw an interesting sight—a field telephone set up! He called the military headquarters at Paoshan and explained our predicament. "All right," they answered, "tomorrow a truck will come out and get you." So that night we slept in the broken truck on the road. The next day we got no farther than Wa Yao—a little restaurant hamlet that catered to the trade of the Burma Road. This, by the way, was where the trail to Lisuland comes out onto the motor road! But Colonel Hsie wished to go to Paoshan first, and so did we in order to buy our staple foods of flour, sugar, and so on. We rightly guessed that the missionaries who had refugeed to our home would have eaten up what we had stored there. And so—the Lord fulfilled His promise and brought me again into that land!

Will I ever forget that vision of Paoshan, swept clean after the destruction! "How doth the city sit solitary that was full of people," were the only words that came. Now I understood why Jeremiah wept and how the lamentation flowed as he sat and beheld Jerusalem's desolations. The business section was laid flat as a plowed field; silence reigned there, and grass was sprouting in the main street.

But Dr. Mei's Medical Unit gave us a warm welcome, with opportunities to preach in the hospital and to the soldiers. Some of the Paoshan Christians still in the city were hungry for fellowship. We learned that, with the exception of one paralytic, not a Christian was killed in that awful bombing, although at least one of them was right on the main street at the time. Praying hard, she crawled under a culvert and was saved. Our hearts went out to those who were left, but God was taking care of them—army personnel were constantly coming and going, so business was good!

We were on our way to dinner with Shao Lao-si one afternoon when two soldiers, sent by Colonel Hsie, came to say he had obtained horses for us to ride and to carry our goods, and we would leave tomorrow! So began a long slow trek into the Salween Canyon. If we had been by ourselves we would have made better time, but Colonel Hsie was in charge and we had to delay when he chose to. It was the rainy season and often we were soaked to the skin, but we had good places to stay at night.

We stopped a day at Six Treasuries where Colonel Hsie left us. This was the home of three feudal

lairds who entertained the colonel to more than food.
I was invited out by the lairds' ladies, to whom I
preached whenever I had opportunity. That last
afternoon while I was away, and Eva was alone,
Colonel Hsie appeared and tried to make love to
her, offering her a college education if she would
go to him! Poor child! She darted past him, ran
out onto the veranda, where at least she could be
heard if she screamed, then faced him and told him
what she thought of him. And Eva, aroused, did
not mince words.

You can imagine our feelings when we returned
and she told us. What a beginning for John, who
was Colonel Hsie's "adviser"! Needless to say, behind our backs the colonel turned our enemy, but
God wonderfully protected us, for he was never
allowed to do us harm.

And now I was to be *home* tomorrow! By nature
I disliked travel and change, and here I had been
tossed from pillar to post for six weary months. I
could hardly wait to get home, to my quiet bedroom by the side of the deep ravine where the
birds sang matins in the morning, and the great
peaks glowed back the sunset hues with their steady
unshakableness at day's end. I longed to get my roots
down comfortably into familiar places! And this,
my last little candleflame had to be blown out.

I had forgotten that the Paoshan refugee missionaries must necessarily have changed things. Believing like us, that Yunnan would fall and the Kuhns
would never return, they had used our things as
they would not have if they had expected to return
them. Outside, home looked just as usual, but inside everything was changed around. Nothing
seemed to be as I had left it, and I felt like a

stranger under my own roof. It seemed as if my last little candleflame of human love had been extinguished. The superintendency had taken my husband (no matter where we lived he would be away from home much of the time); war had taken my girlie; marriage had taken my Lisu helper; and now home was no longer home; my roots couldn't sink down and be comfortable. This seemed to be the last straw that broke the camel's back. To my utter shame, my inner feelings were revealed to those dear guests, and I had to apologize and ask their forgiveness. They did forgive me, but I never forgave myself.

> The sun went down in clouds,
> The moon was darkened by a misty doubt,
> The stars of heaven were dimmed by earthly fears
> And all my little candleflames burned out:
> But while I sat in shadow, wrapped in night
> The face of Christ made all the darkness light.
> —A. J. FLINT

And now, lest you think my dear Master was too hard on me, I want to point out some things. The difficult lessons of 1942 taught me to *fear* leaning heavily on human props. I had surrendered husband, child, friends, all I possesed, long ago. But this was something deeper. This was relinquishing *my rights* to them. This was holding them, but on the open palm of my hand. (Mrs. McFarlane, principal of our language school in Yangchow and a dear warrior saint, had taught me that metaphor. She said, "Keep your treasures on the *open* palm of your hand. If you hold something tight clenched in your fist, God may have to hurt you in order to open your fingers and take it from you. But if it is offered on the *open palm* of your hand, you will hardly know when it is gone." I never found it so easy that I did not *feel* when my treasures were taken, but it did make a tremendous difference. It prevented me from collapsing or sprawling.)

Miss Hannah Hurnard in *Hinds' Feet on High Places* expressed this truth in a different way. Little Much-Afraid, says her beautiful allegory, longed to go with the Shepherd to the High Places. She goes through many trials to get there; the final and greatest is a descent into a steep canyon called the Grave. In this deep valley were an altar and a priest, and here she was asked to let the priest reach into her heart and pull out the plant called *Natural Affection*, root and branch. When I read that I nodded my head with delighted recognition. That was what happened to me in 1942 *"when all my little candleflames burned out."*

It does not mean that after such an experience all affection is gone. Just the very opposite is true. But affection *in its natural state* is dealt with. Affection, especially with intense natures, as it comes to us from Adam, *runs to excess* if given free rein. 'They that are Christ's have crucified the affections and lusts [strong desires]," said Paul (Gal. 5:24).

Uncrucified love runs to inordinate affection and selfish possessiveness which blights rather than blesses. Little Much-Afraid gave up the plant of Natural Affection but she had already received the plant of the Lord's love in her heart. When we allow the Lord to nail our affections to the cross (to use the scriptural metaphor), we do not cease to love. We love even more widely, but it is a love stripped of corrupting influences. Love is not killed— only the seed of corruption in natural affection is killed.

To go back to the practical illustration. When the little candleflames of human joy were allowed to burn out, it hurt. So when God gave me a new one, presenting Eva to me, I was immediately on my guard. *Natural affection* would have prompted me to so embrace her that we became all-in-all to one another. *Crucified affection* caused me to love her but always be alert that it might never become *inordinate affection.* Always I reminded myself, "The time will come that I must do without her. How should we live so when that time comes, we can each separate without being *undone?*" That is, never to let the other one become indispensable, so that when the human prop is removed, there is a painful sprawl. Never to let *home* become so indispensable that at His call I cannot give it up! This brought me into a realm of unexpected freedom and relaxation. Human loves did not cease to delight but they no longer enslaved. Now I do not want to profess that from the year 1942 on I never again defaulted in this matter of enslaving affections. I defaulted often enough to keep me humble and totally cast upon the Lord. I cannot even sustain the lesson I learned, without His help! My own strength is entirely untrustworthy. But through the experiences of 1942 I received a wholesome *fear* of what disobedience would do to me. And that fear helped to keep me looking to Him.

Crucified affections lift you into a realm of childlike simplicity and relaxation. "Except ye become as little children," warned our Lord, "ye shall not enter the kingdom of heaven" (Matt. 18:3). The little child takes each day as it comes. He does not waste time imagining tomorrow's woes. He lives a day at a time. If today has tears, they are shed and spent; but they are not carried over into tomorrow. In the days that were to be ahead of me, I would again have partings and separations from loved ones that cost heart agony for some hours. But never again did they overwhelm me. In other words, all the suffering when my little candleflames went out, one after the other, were worth the tears they cost, for they purchased for me a permanent freedom from sprawling spiritually, from being knocked down and overwhelmed.

In other words, it was a kind Lord, and not a vicious One who blew out my candles, systematically, one after the other. He had something better for me than earthly candles.

> And as I sat in shadow, wrapped in night
> The face of Christ made all the darkness light.

As I look back on 1942, the disappointments and heartaches are a dark blur. That which stands out was the unfailing faithfulness of my Lord. When I was kicking against the pricks, He was never impatient, never withdrew His love. Every time I cried to Him to fulfill the promise of Genesis 28:15 He responded immediately. *"The power of his resurrection"*—that is what stands out most sharply. And the dearness of Himself—*"that I may know him."*

And now see what He was lovingly planning to give me as soon as my Job-experience had borne fruit. He did not even wait for that fruition, but gave me Eva as a foretaste. And a wonderful reception back to Lisuland from our dear spiritual children. I could not even imagine that in a year's time a little baby son with red-gold hair and snow-white skin would be cuddled in my arms. It was beyond thought that our home should be moved from Oak

Flat and that I would be put down right beside
Lucius and Mary in the Village of Olives. Yet that
is what happened. And there I had not only Lucius
and Mary, but Eva and Danny as well! And my dear
girlie was repatriated on the *Gripsholm*, and until
we could get back to her, she was taken into the
home of old friends—Mr. and Mrs. George Sutherland, who became her foster parents. When we
had to return to the field, they took her back and
loved her as their own child. Unthinkable kind-
nesses. But just like Him.

These plans of my dear Lord were all piled up
waiting for me, just around the corner of the future.
And He who was so lovingly dear to me will be
the same to you.

> One cannot pierce the curtain
>   Across the path ahead,
> But one can be quite certain
>   That on the road we tread
> The Father's love will guide us;
>   His everlasting arms
> Will guard and keep and hide us
>   From all that truly harms.
>   —UNKNOWN

CHAPTER SEVEN

SMALL HARASSMENTS

UP TO NOW we have seen the Lord making Himself known through wondrous workings. The sneering unbeliever would call them coincidences perhaps. But the child of God, watching the exact timing, the quick reply to a sudden prayer, does not hesitate to label them miracles. It is a miracle when you can count on it beforehand, without any knowledge of how it would possibly happen.

But there is a less spectacular platform whereon God also manifests Himself. It is one of everyday struggle with every day's small problems. Nothing breath-taking has happened. Yet at the end of the year, or after a long period has passed, as one thoughtfully reviews it, suddenly one sees it. "Look!" we say. "Wasn't it a miracle that with all that was against us, we were enabled to go steadily forward?" It is the forward pushing, despite the harassment of small trials that prick, sting, and weary one. And perhaps this is the platform which God uses most often in the average Christian's life. So we want to look at its possibilities.

The Kuhns were now back in the canyon, although John must still keep his travel circuit as superintendent of the Chinese churches along the Burma Road. From the military point of view we were in the danger zone (civilians were not allowed past Tali City without a military pass). Some Japanese were just across the mountains from us, and some of them just across the Salween River but several days' journey to the south. Colonel Hsie and his guerillas had prepared trenches along the east bank of the Salween. (Oak Flat Village is on the east bank but 2,000 feet above the river.) Later, the colonel and his men moved over to Village of the Olives which is on the west bank. Of course, they had spies out all the time, and no one was allowed to cross the river without a military pass. The Japanese were known to be in the area of the great pass into Burma, the vicinity of which can be seen from our porch at Oak Flat, so we were never allowed to forget them.

Our winter schedule was usually to travel among the villages holding a two-weeks' Bible study wherever we were invited. But this year of 1942 the Rainy Season Bible School had had to be shortened owing to the paratyphoid which had broken out among the staff. So they had decided to hold the third month's study in October, by which time the weather had cleared, and the missionaries had recovered. This decision, in the Lord's kind providence, gave me the opportunity of teaching our beloved RSBS student group. John was with us only for the beginning of the school, as he had to go out to Chinaland to escort Dr. Mei's Medical Unit. These were coming to Lisuland for a couple of weeks' free medical ministry to the Lisu tribe.

Those days the whole world was learning from England what a boost to a nation's morale is the spirit of *blitz or no blitz, we carry on business as usual!* The Christian missionary surely should have equal courage and faith. This was the reason we

decided to ignore the *danger zone* and go quietly
on with our usual program. It had a wonderfully
stabilizing effect upon the whole countryside, for
the Lisu were jittery at the presence of so many
armed men and ready to desert their villages for
caves and other places of refuge high in the mountains.

October dawned beautifully sunny, and a fine
group of students assembled. But the school had
barely started when word came that the soldiers in
a strange uniform, one hundred strong, had arrived
at the stream north of Cow's Hump Village. This
threw everyone into panic. The Lisu, who had never
seen a Japanese, suspected every strange uniform,
and these soldiers were Orientals, they declared.

My diary says it was a Saturday when this dis-
turbing news reached us. And on Saturdays we had
no classes, for our students were sent into the surrounding villages to evangelize or to conduct Sunday services. One of the Lisu came in to tell us
that our Oak Flat villagers were packing up for
flight. Mrs. Yang and her mother had already
gone to a hamlet difficult of access far in the ravine,
and others had fled to their fields. Cow's Hump was
a long day's march to the north of us, but Oak
Flat was so close to the main road down the canyon
that plunderers certainly would not pass us by.

The next day, Sunday, was calm and sunny. It
was the custom for Christians in the nearby villages
to come to Oak Flat chapel for worship, but with
this scary rumor abroad we wondered how many
would dare to come! It is easy for Lisu, however,
with nothing to carry to skip up the mountainside
like wild goats and, if the need arises, disappear
even as you look at them. So that Sunday noon saw

several hundred arrive to worship. The missionaries still at their post had sent word that the Bible
school would continue as usual. Students who had
gone to villages close at hand for the weekend would
be expected to report for school by Sunday evening,
and everyone was supposed to be back by nine
o'clock Monday morning for classes. This word,
carried back home to the villages scattered over peak
and ridge, had a stabilizing effect upon everyone. So
it was no surprise later to hear that the students who
had gone north toward Cow's Hump had returned
with the news *that the strange soldiers were not
Japanese!* They were Chinese from Honan province
with a slightly different uniform and accent. What
they were doing in the canyon was unexplained, but
fears were dispelled sufficiently for classes to resume
again on Monday morning.

By Monday evening more *wind-words* blew to us.
The strange soldiers had burned Beheaded Tribes-
man's Village! That was bad news, but at least it
told us that they were headed for the Mekong Valley and were not coming down our way. We had
had a peaceful day of study.

By Tuesday the matter was cleared up. The soldiers were a group of deserters; they had not really
burned any village, just plundered a bit, and now
they were gone. So our little Bible school breathed
freely once more and continued on calmly until its
scheduled end. If we had all fled that Saturday night,
and Sunday worshipers had found the missionary
staff in hiding, the students would have fled in alarm
to their own homes, and the school would have fallen
apart. I wonder too, if later schools, challenged to
come under even more dangerous conditions, would

have had the confidence to do so. This was to be our periodic temptation for the next two years. "Business as usual?—Impossible." "Well, let us stick to it as long as we can, and then see what God does for us." Under that spirit we were to prove Him in a quiet but thrilling way on the Platform of Small Harassments.

Life proceeded rather smoothly until the next February. The Japanese did not seem to be gaining, and Colonel Hsie crossed the Salween and talked of occupying Fort Pien Ma. But at the Christmas festival when I had asked for an estimate of how many girls planned to come to our yearly Girls' Bible School in February, not one would promise! Taxes were high now and war rumors unsettling. The Lisu work is indigenous, so of course the students all paid their own way, except for the wives of the evangelists, whose board was paid by the church. But even these wives would only say they "hoped" they could come! "What if we came and then the military situation deteriorated suddenly and we could not get back again across the river?" they asked. We had no answer. That could easily happen; we could only pray the Lord to restrain the enemy so that the girls of the church might have this opportunity for Bible study which came only once a year for them.

But as 1943 dawned and all seemed quiet, there came the question, "Should we prepare for a girls' school without the promise of even one scholar?" The dormitories were badly in need of repair—they were leaking and leaning off the plumb—and the beds had disappeared. It would cost money to repair them and time to oversee the job. Who would take the responsibility of ordering it?

Charles Peterson (at this time a bachelor) was the missionary in charge of Oak Flat station in 1943. I was to assist him where I could and John also, when he was home. Charles and I prayed about it and decided to live during these war days as if life were normal. "Business as usual" was to be our motto as well as that of London blitz endurers. If we were not to hold a scheduled school, we felt the Lord would warn us ahead of time. If He did not say "stop!" was it not common sense to infer that He meant go ahead? So we decided to have the dormitories repaired and, as Charles would be out in the village holding Bible classes, I had to hire the workmen and oversee the job.

There was also another kind of preparation needed. Always we tried to have new hymns and choruses translated for the girls so that they might have an interesting contribution to make in their home villages when they finished their studies. The girl students would be asked to teach the other Christians in their villages anything new there was to be learned. It was not usual for Lisu women to stand up and teach, so they needed strong encouragement to be induced to even try. A bright new chorus was excellent bait, and the girls soon forgot their self-consciousness when they discovered that their audience was eager to learn what they alone could teach. So both girls and the Christian villagers were helped by the subjects taught at Girls' Bible School.

Our circular of those days explains John's absence that February: "Hubby is off on high adventure—trying to rescue Mr. and Mrs. Fred Hatton, who are still behind the Japanese lines at Stockade Hill." As a matter of fact, he was not successful in a rescue but as superintendent he was responsible to try. But this meant that Charles and I must carry on without him.

But as the day for assembling at Girls' Bible School drew near, the weather turned against us. Snow clouds came down over the great peaks (12—15,000 feet high), the wind blew icy cold, and on the lower slopes the snow turned to rain—wet, penetrating, chill, damp. These storm spells in February sometimes continued for two weeks. The girls on the west bank of the Salween would have over twenty miles of mountain road to travel, besides crossing a dangerous river; they would not dare attempt it in a snowstorm.

Saturday was assembling day and by night we had over a dozen girls, but all from the east bank. Now our most progressive students (mentally and spiritually) were those who lived on the west bank, so you can imagine how we prayed for them to come.

Sunday continued stormy. But Monday there was a lull. It did not really clear—the sky was dull and gray all day— but at least there was no downpour. Would the girls attempt to come? We could not know until evening so we began the school with the girls we had.

You can imagine our thrill at sunset when a shout came ringing up the trail, "Girls from the west bank are coming!"

We ran to the door, and there around the edge of the mountain was a line of little dots moving down the trail toward us! Sure enough. We ran out gingerly, for the ground was too wet and slippery to allow speed, and on to the Oak Flat trail which connects with the main road up and down the canyon. There they were—their bedding and books in big bags slung over their shoulders or carried on the back with the strap placed over the forehead to distribute the weight. Mary, Lydia, Julia, Chloe—and their brothers or husbands coming on behind, carrying their grain supply! Happy smiles and handshakes. "We were afraid you wouldn't make it," was answered by a chorus of girlish exclamations as to the difficulties encountered and their determination to press through. Chatter, chatter as bare feet pattered over the muddy trails to the church kitchen where warm fires and a hot supper were waiting.

That night, for the first evening session of the school, we had thirty-three students! And what a praise service! How it pays to take one step at a time with God! What if we had not prepared the dormitories? That very night the storm descended again and kept it up for a week. God's children need courage as well as faith. Courage to begin preparations for the workings of God: clearing the deck for action, so to speak. For sometimes His door opens only for a very short period, and if one is not fully ready to enter in, it will close perhaps permanently. There was only that one lull in the bad weather (that Monday morning) for a week or more.

With so many bright-faced girls to teach, Charles, Eva, and I swung into the schoolwork with joy and zest, despite bitter cold and sloppy mountain trails. We thought our harassments were conquered, but alas, *no*.

The second or third day of the school Charles appeared (I think we were changing classes, I coming out and he going in to teach) with a gloomy face.

"Guess what, Isobel! Old Fox's Chinese scribe is here with the *thief!* He took the whole last hour

of my preparation time which I had planned to spend
on this lesson I have to teach now! I'm not sure what
he is after—he's down there waiting for you now.
Do pray for me this hour! I did so want to give my
best," and then he disappeared into the classroom.

I proceeded downhill with a sinking heart. *Fox*
was the nickname we had given to the local feudal
laird because of his sly ways. The thief was a heathen
neighbor who lived over the hill from us and who
had robbed us one night while we were at church.
He was a notorious robber, but as he shared his
spoils with the Fox and the Fox's scribe, they protected him. We had lost about two hundred dollars
(Chinese) in cash and some clothing—a green sweater of mine, being one article. John, with some com-
panions, had accidently walked into a Lisu house
and found Mr. Thief seated at the friend's fire wearing *Isobel's green sweater!* He had no chance to
escape and the native official with John said, "Leave
him to me. I'll see he gets impounded—you proceed
on your journey." There was nothing else for John
to do, apparently. Usually it was not our practice to
take the Lisu to law: and fervently did I wish it
had not been done now.

I found the scribe and his retinue (dirty, greasy
half-breeds they were, who had studied Chinese
and spoke it with such a strong tribal accent that
I could hardly recognize it as Chinese, which added
to my difficulties). I too had planned on using the
next hour for study preparation. I had added some
mother-craft subjects to those usually taught in Girls'
Bible School and I needed to look up some Lisu
expressions not often used outside of a dictionary
or a delivery room. And here were these four broadly
grinning men bowing before me and apparently

enjoying themselves. Moreover, it was ten o'clock, the hour such men expect to be served breakfast! I bowed, asked them to be seated, then turned around to call Eva. She was right there. Her class (knitting and babycraft sewing) was in the afternoon so fortunately she was free.

"Don't worry, Ma-ma," she whispered. "I saw they intended to eat here, and I've got a meal almost ready for them. In just five minutes!"

Was there ever such a jewel of a girl? What would I have done without her? And wherever would she get meat to feed them with? Their social rank was such that they would be insulted if they were not served meat dishes. There was no place where we could buy meat. At the laird's castle, of course, they slaughtered for their own use almost every day. For ourselves we found chicken the easiest to obtain. If it was skinny we boiled it for stew and so on. But soon the meat was on the table. (Eva had mixed a bit of bacon with this vegetable, a bit of leftover chicken with that one, and today's chicken in another form made a third dish. For culinary art, Eva deserved a medal!)

Of course they ate at great leisure and I, as their hostess, could not leave them. And you do not discuss business at mealtime. I saw my first hour go, and my second hour for preparation about to be invaded, before the scribe sat back and explained his errand.

He told me he had the thief chained and handcuffed in the village in another house. Then he began to extol Christianity—praising us with flattery that was detestable to me, knowing that he himself spurned the Lord. On and on he went, but I was baffled—what was he driving at? Did I need to sign a document accusing the thief? I knew that Orientals do not "come to the point" as we forthright Americans like to do, but I really could not guess his purpose in praising us for our big-heartedness, our gfood deeds, our forgiving spirit. As the second hour was drawing to a close I determined to end it—etiquette or no etiquette!

"I'm sorry, but we have a school here this month," I explained, "and my duties call me away. Was there something you wanted me to sign?"

"Oh, no"—how very broad became the grins now. "Then Mrs. Kuhn would be able to meet them this afternoon? Would she name the hour? Maybe she wished to *see* the thief?"

Oh, no, I had no such desire. It was all a miserable business to me. But they were waiting for an answer. Four o'clock in the afternoon? At Mr. Peterson's cabin? (Maybe he could help me understand their garbled Chinese.) And with that they bowed themselves out, still grinning broadly.

Now I had to catch up broken threads. The mimeograph work on the new chorus was not yet finished perhaps. Clutching at the fleeing moments so to speak, I saw one of the Lisu deacons crossing my path and called him. We talked as we climbed toward the classroom together.

"Tell me quick, Deacon A," I said, "what is the scribe here for? Has he come to return the money? Should I sign something?"

"Oh, no, Ma-ma," replied the Lisu. "The thief invested all the $200.00 he stole from you in cotton cloth meaning to sell it on the market. When the Fox heard about the robbery, he just hauled in the cloth. He's got it now, down in his yamen. The scribe will get part of it, but you won't get any—

and the thief hopes to get free, that's all he'll get."

"But isn't there any justice in —?" I was still sputtering when we reached the classroom and I had to leave the deacon and go in.

We were harassed by the scribe and his men for two days and a half. Finally, the scribe felt that Mrs. Kuhn was just too stupid to ever get the point: he would have to break all etiquette and be frank with her! So leaning forward he said, "Mrs. Kuhn, this man's record is so bad that if I put your accusation on paper I will then have to send him across to Luchang to the Chinese government magistrate. Only that magistrate has the power to sentence to death. And he has said that if the thief offended once more, he would have him killed. So then if you compel me to put his accusation on paper you will be the cause of his death. You're a Christian missionary. Do you want that? Christianity professes love and forgiveness."

"Oh, yes," I answered, light having been broken so clearly for me. "But Christianity does not condone sin! I will forgive him, but he should return the money he stole."

"Oh, he spent that long ago. There's none of it left," said the scribe shaking with laughter. "Isn't that so?" he inquired of his three henchmen.

Oh, how they laughed! Yes, yes, they assured Mrs. Kuhn, that was all gone long ago. Not a cent of it left! He would return the green sweater, and Mrs. Kuhn would magnanimously forgive him. Wonderful thing Christianity—grin, grin, grin.

By this time the thief himself had been brought in. He squatted at my feet watching this dramatic scene with mild interest, but with absolutely no shame or repentance visible.

"Mr. Y——," I said quietly (inwardly my Irish blood was boiling). "Christianity *is* a wonderful thing. I'd like to explain it a little to you, please." Silence, and four amused pairs of eyes turned on me.

"Christianity teaches that God is no respecter of persons. And He is omniscient—He knows everything, even our thoughts. *He even knows where that cloth is which the thief here bought with the stolen money.* And when we come to die, God is going to judge each of us according to our acceptance of His Son the Lord Jesus or our rejection. He will not ask, Who is the scribe for the the laird, and, Who is the thief in prison. He will ask, *Did you accept the provision I made for your salvation,* or did you reject it? If you rejected it, you will go to Hell just the same as the thief here. You will be on a level there— rejecters of the Christ of God. I earnestly exhort you not to neglect so great salvation. In the eyes of the Judge of all the earth, you are as bad as he is right now."

The atmosphere of the cabin had changed. There were no more grins, but in place of merriment four red-faced and ashamed heads hung down. The scribe muttered something about "entering the church by and by," got up, and said they must go. One pair of eyes *did* twinkle—those of the thief. But he was looking at the scribe who carefully avoided noticing him.

I was given the green sweater, the thief asked me to forgive him, which I did, and the four half- breeds walked out and left us at peace, at last.

How did we ever get through those days? We did not know. But when all was over, and we compared notes, we found that no classes had been canceled.

Somehow or other one of us was always able to take over the class when the scribe sent for one of us to come and talk.

The school was a real blessing as was shown by the tears that flowed down the girls' cheeks when they had to say good-by at the end of the month. It was abundantly worth it.

One little anecdote will be interesting to you even if not in direct connection with our theme. Six years had passed, and in that time I never again saw the scribe. At length one day I heard one Lisu call out to another, "The scribe is waiting for you at Ni-do—he says to meet him there." I looked up.

"Why doesn't the scribe come here for it?" I asked idly. "I haven't seen him in a long time."

The Lisu in front of me stared at me. "Don't you know, Ma-ma? Honestly don't you know why the scribe never comes to Oak Flat any more?"

So I was right: deliberately he had been avoiding an encounter.

"No, I don't know," I replied. "What is it?"

"He says he is afraid of *Yang-si-muh*"—my Chinese surname and title.

The February Girls' Bible School safely accomplished, what was next on the program for 1943? We had written down a new venture—a short Bible school for teen-age boys. These are usually the family cowhands, but of course we did not wish to limit it to that class, so we just announced a Boys' Bible School in March—for ten- to twenty-year olds. At the Christmas festival we had announced it, and drew the attention of Christian families to the date set. Plowing had not yet begun and so other members of the family would be free to watch the cattle and let the cowherd come to this school if we held it in March.

Cows and bulls are used in plowing the steep mountainside and often represent the investment of the family earnings. On such precipitous slopes the cattle can easily get to fighting and push one another over the ridge. They must be watched all the time. In some places at certain times of the year the cowherd takes the cattle to a dell where the grass is luscious, and camps out there himself, not returning home at night. In other words, it is hard to contact these boys for the Lord. March, 1943, we had written down as our first attempt.

March 6 they were to assemble; on March 4 news came that our postmaster at the town of Six Treasuries had fled and was in hiding because he feared the arrival of the Japanese! Six Treasuries was only one day's distance from us, south on our side of the river. Chinese soldiers were already posted at the two ferry crossings, waiting to destroy those ferries if the Japanese appeared. Suppose some boys from the west bank did come, and the boats were destroyed? They would not be able to get back home.

To add to our harassments, the weather was rainy, and our cook[1] gave notice that he was leaving. His bride of a few weeks was homesick, and Joe must go and live with her people.

We now had had a little experience with the platform of harassments; so we plodded on as if life were normal.

Thirty-six cowherds arrived! And Mr. Yang, the

---

[1]Joe of *Nests Above the Abyss*, p. 236.

principal of the church school,[2] decided to cancel all classes so that his students could also attend, which swelled the number to *seventy-six!*

Before the Boys' Bible School ended, word came that the Japanese had arrived at Pien Ma Pass. Overhead airplanes were seen daily and sometimes even a dog-fight! For we were right under the trail of The Hump flights. But we finished in peace. I quote from our circulars.

> We had a closing-day program for the boys, and the four little cowherds from Lamah Village brought much applause by rendering a beautiful anthem on Psalm 24 *a cappella* and in four parts! Charles Peterson said that one small mannie stood and sang like a bishop! With all the pleasure of it, there were smiles of amusement too.
>
> And after they got home? Lucius said that his cowherd (who had won the honor of being elected Conductor of Music for the occasion) well—his tongue went so fast and so long recounting all his wonderful two weeks at Oak Flat that no one else got a word in edgewise all evening!

So at the end of March we had that good feeling of having attained. A spiritual battle, contested at every step, but now finished—*attained*. Is there a thrill on earth to equal it? Yes, to hear one's spiritual children are walking in the ways of the Lord is akin to it. But these are deep things that pierce far below the surface and send a glowing joy throughout one's being. They give meaning and purpose to

_____

[2]The Chinese school was a church project by which children of Christian Lisu families could study Chinese, taking the regular elementary Chinese school curriculum. They were not taught much Bible or Lisu script so Mr. Yang felt they should take advantage of the Boys' Bible School.

life and they bring the thread of eternal value into the pattern, not visible before. In other words, God has revealed Himself to us afresh in small harassments and we are forever enriched by it.

Maybe the harassment is too earthly to call a platform. Not only earthly but ridiculous. These can be like the last straw on the camel's back—the culminating sting of frustration that just seems more than we can take. Yet it is so puny we dare not list it among our trials. Take, for instance, the careless laziness of our goatherd.

Milk was a necessity, especially when Daniel Kreadman Kuhn appeared August 1, 1943. It was soon obvious that Mother's milk must be supplemented. That year, in that distant corner, powdered milk or even canned milk was out of sight in price. The hillside was too steep for cows, so a herd of goats furnished our milk. But never could we get a competent goatherd. He would only milk as much as he felt like—a quart today, a cup tomorrow! He would deny that more than a cup was to be squeezed from the critter! Neither Eva nor I knew how to milk so we could not prove our point. Exasperation!

Also, he would not even herd the animals carefully. We had two billies. The older we called *Hitler,* because he loved to rule and had a passion for destruction. He became quite rambunctious as he saw the younger billy growing up and able to hold his own; this made him want to be first in all things. When they were being driven home at night, the older billy would frequently rush ahead of the herd and make for our kitchen. Woe betide the cook if the door were not securely fastened! Hitler would rush in and make for the garbage pail. Being so big and strong he was difficult to handle in that small place where a hard kick could dent the pots or break the bowls. But one day he waxed bolder—he found the stairs to the grain storeroom.

I was in my bedroom working at my desk when I heard noises. Push—bang—a yell in Chinese—a loud whack—a squeal, then a terrific commotion. Above it all arose Eva's voice, high with anger: "Ma-ma! Big Goat Old Man" (she could not stop to remember the correct English for the *older billy*, and Hitler was attached to him after this event), "Big Goat Old Man go storeroom! Make awful mess!" When Eva got excited, English grammar flew to the winds—nouns and verbs were mainly all that were needed. I got up and went out to behold a spectacle.

There was Big Goat Old Man running for his life up the hill toward the refuge of his pen. After him was a blur of blue Chinese gown and a stick that ascended and descended regularly—on hair or on air—up and down it went. I laughed until I cried. He who lorded it so over the females of the goat pen was scurrying in ignominy ahead of one small dot of femininity from Chinaland. There is no question as to who won that battle!

Nor is there any question as to how harassing a messed-up storeroom can be when Bible school is in session. We must either discipline ourselves to leave it alone until we have time to sweep and tidy it, or we must give up some hoped-for leisure time and do it. In any case it leads to self-discipline and this is a place where we meet the Lord.

"*A soul well-disciplined is beyond all price,*" (Knox's Translation). I have met the Lord here many times. Philippians 3:21 used to be a help to me. It says that He is able to subdue *all* things unto Himself. When the hot feelings of rebellion against

circumstances would storm up in my heart I have
often cried to Him, "Lord, Thou saidst *all* things,
that must mean me. Then *subdue me*, subdue this
flaming resentment, O Lord, I pray Thee." And
then He would, but first He met me and it was on
just such a humiliating platform—a small harassment.

*　*　*

The fact that the Rainy Season Bible School of
1942 had to be broken into two sessions by the
paratyphoid sickness among the white staff gave
the idea to the Lisu church of breaking it up into
three sessions of one month each for 1943. This did
not prove as satisfying, but it certainly was of the
Lord for that year. I had told no one but John
that we were expecting baby Danny to arrive in
August; which would of course, have meant that
I could not help in teaching. But the church voted
that for 1943 RSBS be held in three sessions, April,
August, and November.

Unknown to us, God was planning to call Mrs.
Leila Cooke Home to Himself in May just before
the RSBS at Luda began their three months' study.
Our change of schedule enabled Charles Peterson
to teach our students in April, then go up to Luda
and help teach there for some two months or more,
and still he could be back at Oak Flat for the November session of our school. John took the main burden of teaching our RSBS in August but in the
middle of September he had to leave. I had no doctor's help with Danny's advent but one of our CIM
nurses, Miss Dorothy Burrows, skilled in obstetrics,
generously offered to take her annual vacation by
coming to the canyon and playing doctor for me.
She stayed with me for more than a month after the

confinement, but as she was serving on the Tali Hospital Staff, she had to get back to work, and must have an escort out. (Colonel Hsie had escorted her in—he going out for consultation and to get new supplies.) So John escorted Dorothy to Tali and then went on to Chungking where the CIM Superintendents' Conference was to assemble. This left only Charles and me for the November session of RSBS at Oak Flat.

John and my dear nurse had no sooner disappeared than harassment arrived! Danny developed a need for a new milk formula, warning of which he could not speak to us, of course, so he just cried—all the time. This was the first installment of trouble. The circular of those days tells more:

> They had left us but one day when Charles came down with what turned out to be rheumatic fever! At the same time our goatherd took sick and also the girl who does the laundry.
> And the rain came down!
> Then I got word that Colonel Hsie with his number two wife was coming through, which I supposed meant that we must entertain them! What I would do without Eva's help, I didn't know.

Charles' cabin was down the mountain from ours, and all his meals had to be carried to him. I have memories of trying to carry his tray down that slippery path, the rain drizzling on me, and my hands shaking with weakness—I was so tired from sleepless nights with Danny. And the November Bible school looming up on the horizon! Should we call it off? It semed utterly impossible that we could hold it! Then we reminded each other that this was beginning to be a chronic state with our Bible school plans! Impossible to hold it! And yet God had seen us through every time we had stepped out in faith, and tried to do it.

As we prayed together, light came. Charles said to me, "There is Orville Carlson at Luda. He has not been in the work very long, but he is quick at the language and he taught in the Luda RSBS. He could surely help teach our November session. I helped Mr. Cooke. I'm sure they would lend Orville to us. Maybe he could come early and help nurse me." So a messenger was dispatched to Luda to explain our predicament and ask for Orville Carlson. In the meantime—well, Charles and I laugh over the memory of one grim evening.

It was a Sunday, Eva had gone to church. I was going to go to bed early but had a feeling that I should go down to Charles' cabin first and see if he needed any help. He did. The rheumatic fever was getting under way now, and he was in such pain that he needed a shot of morphine. So back up the slippery path I went to sterilize the hypodermic needle. Behold, the charcoal fire in the kitchen was almost out. With much blowing and coaxing I got a few coals hot enough to boil it the ten minutes required. Then down the mountainside I went again with the pot and needle. But I had never given an injection before this as John had always done it for me. Charles was suffering yet I hated to experiment on him. I felt I must confess my inexperience to him.

"Oh, it's easy," said Charles, picking up the needle and fitting it into the syringe. "You just want to be sure there is no bubble," and to show me how, he held the syringe up, pressed the plunger and shot my carefully sterilized needle through the open window into the wet mud of the dark mountainside!

I had no other needle so had to take a lantern and search for that one. Then I trudged up the mountain to our kitchen only to find that the fire was out! I forgot what happened after that. Probably church was dismissed and Eva came to my rescue, for lighting charcoal fires was never where I shone! My first lesson in giving an injection!

"Oh, it's easy. All you do is—shoot it out the window!"

Small harassments; they come to everyone. What are we to do with them or *in* them? Seek a promise from the Lord. Nothing is too small but that He will respond to comfort or to guide. My diary says that His Word to me those days was Psalm 44:4: *"Thou art my King, O God: command deliverances for Jacob."*

"When did I licht ma auld lantern?" asked a Scotch deacon. "Was it no when I was comin' frae the licht o' ma ain hoose along the dark road tae the licht o' yours? That is where tae use the promises—*in the dark places between the lichts."* Stumbling down the mountainside in the rain with a tray for a sick fellow worker—from *ma hoose tae your hoose*—that is where to use your light.

"Thou art my King, O God: command deliverances." He does not rule out small harassments; but He does rule that they shall not *overcome* us! And they didn't.

Orville arrived in due time.

Colonel Hsie and wife two also arrived; but as he planned that she stay indefinitely at Oak Flat Village, he took over the Clinic House and set her up there, with her own household establishment. They were no trouble to me.

And baby Dan's crying spells at night? I soon was

using goat's milk to supplement nursing him. But I could find no formula for goat's milk and as it has a heavier curd than cow's milk, Danny had much colic—that is why he cried so. But dear little Eva insisted on also lifting this burden from me. I would never *ask* anybody to take over my baby at night—that was my responsibility, I felt. But I didn't have to ask. As soon as he awoke and raised his voice in protest at colic pains, Eva could hear him, for there were only bamboo walls between us. Soon there was a patter of small feet down the hall and a knock at my door.

"Give him to me, Ma-ma," says Eva's voice. "I've got the charcoal fire going and his milk is warm," and off she would trot with him. What magic she used I do not know, but in less than an hour, back she would come with a sound-asleep little bundle, comforted. She knew how to bury hot coals in a brazier and then blow them up again into a hot fire. I tried to learn how (to save Eva's self-imposed night labor), but all I ever succeeded in doing was to blow the ashes all over the bedroom, nearly choke myself with them, and completely kill whatever coals had ever been alive! At last I gave up trying and allowed Eva to make her nightly excursion down the hall. Oh, you will wonder why I did not use a vacuum bottle. Ours broke and there was no place near where I could get another. So, you see, God *was* my King, and He *did* command deliverances for this poor Jacob. And again He had proved that in harassments was a good place to get to *know Him!*

* * *

Before 1944 dawned, the Japanese had entered the Salween Canyon! Colonel Hsie's bringing his wife to live in our village was because he foresaw this, but of course it also put us in the most dangerous limelight.

With the enemy right across the river from us (we stood and watched the town of Luchang go up in flames, as the Japanese fired it). Surely now we could not keep a normal schedule! Especially when the year's program began with the *Girls'* Bible School. The girls would never have the faith and courage to come, for one thing, would they? But the past two years of quietly carrying on our normal projects had unconsciously been training the Lisu church (as well as ourselves) in the power of God to give victory on the platform of harassments. To tell the truth, I was inwardly hoping the girls would not come! Isn't that confession?

But Charles Peterson had been sent out to civilization for a three months' sick rest, and, although my own dear John was with me this time, did he not come down with influenza! I also had a baby to care for and altogether as I faced the Girls' Bible School my courage oozed away—and I fear it pulled faith with it!

But is it not wonderful that *when we are faithless, He abideth faithful?* (II Tim. 2:13). He knew that really and truly in the bottom of my heart I wanted that Girls' Bible School.

They came—twenty-five of them, and the bright ones from the west bank among them! And what a good time we had, despite more harassments. (Baby caught the flu from John and then I caught it!)

GBS was accomplished; thank Thee, Lord! What's next on the program? Oh, Boys' Bible School. But this time it *truly* is impossible. (Each test became a little severer than the last one.)

John had to leave on March 9 for Chungking—yearly conference of CIM superintendents.

Charles was not yet back from sick-leave. I would be the only white missionary on the staff. Eva did not have sufficient training to teach boys (they, of course, were not interested in knitting, etc.).

And we were out of writing materials (pencils, scribblers, paper, and ink). I had ordered them, but the Japanese were on one road in between us and Paoshan (the city where we purchased our supplies) and fear that they would cross over to the only remaining road made carriers unwilling to make the trip.

Try to have a Bible school with only one teacher and possibly no writing materials? Wasn't that impossible? But the Lisu church surprised me. This adventuring with God was revealing a new joy and zest to them. To my astonishment I found the church leaders were *in consternation* lest Ma-ma cancel the school!

"Oh, ho," I said to myself. "All right, my lads." To them I said, "I will trust God for the writing supplies, if the Lisu church will consent to set free two of the trained evangelists from their village pastoral duties to come and help me teach."

They withdrew to consult over that and returned beaming. "We consent," they said, "and we have appointed Teachers Luke Fish and Thomas Hemp[3] to help you teach; they will be excused from other duties during March." So the school was announced.

But the enemy of souls had not exhausted his

---

[3]These are the Luke Fish and Thomas Hemp whose pictures are in *Nests Above the Abyss.*

repertoire of harassments. Assembly day came and—
no writing supplies; but also—*no Teacher Thomas
and no boys from the west bank of the Salween!*
Thomas was pastor across the river. Luke was pastor on Oak Flat Mountain where we lived. Luke
and I faced each other in dismay that evening.

"It's persecution," said Luke grimly. And I had
felt the same. It required a military pass to get
across the river, as we have said. There had been
no difficulty about this before, as John was officially
personnel adviser to the general. (Colonel Hsie was
now a general.) But a new personality had appeared
on the scene—a Chinese small official had been
sent to the west bank of the Salween to teach Chinese
to Lisu young people and to recruit Lisu young men
for the military school in Tali City. I did not know
that the granting of west bank passes to cross the
Salween was now in this man's hands. But from
his peculiar efforts to win over the *Christian* young
people, I had suspected him of being a Red infil-
trator. He was. A few years later he was executed
in Kunming as a Communist spy. But this was 1943,
and we had no proofs of anything.

There was nothing to do but pray; behind it was
Satan, and God is the only one who can deal with
him. So down on our knees we went. Now I will
quote from the circular of that time.

As we prayed for Thomas' release, the Lord
worked! Prepare for a surprise . . . into our home
here drop some *American* soldiers. (Whether they
dropped from the sky or came in by the road, the
censor would not let me tell you.) But after a good
square American meal (the poor fellows had not
seen such food, simple as it is, for a long time, and
wasn't it fun "stuffing" them!) they asked if they

could do anything for us, and as they have *influence*, we got them to pull the proper wire and the evening of the fifth day of school, Thomas arrived. Then blessing avalanched.

Thomas brought Lucius and three pupils with him. There had been eleven who wanted to come, but on refusal of the pass, the others had gone back home.

The morning after we welcomed them, in walk the paper and pencils!

Then, hard on their heels and without warning in comes—Charlie Peterson.

Well, the Boys' Bible School that began with such a limp, ended with a grand flourish. The influx of more teachers meant more individual attention. And the Lisu teachers got practice in doing some things they have never thought they could do. A new chorus was needed, and, as I had not time to compose one, I gave Luke a tune and told him to find the words! He produced a soldier theme and it was a great hit!

Then the task of designing a study certificate had to be laid on his shoulders too. (To get a certificate for only two weeks' study would be a joke in America, but to these boys, many of whom will never again be given the opportunity to study away from home, a certificate will be treasured all their lives.)

Lucius did the drawing, and much of the hand printing on the certificates and they were really pretty!

Charles swung right in, drilled and advised on the closing-day program until it was one of the brightest and most interesting we have had—a glad memory to us all.

Again, on the platform of small harassments, we had met the power of the Lord and came to know

His ability to give the grace of continuance: another school accomplished as per schedule.

RSBS in 1944 was held during the summer in comparative quiet as the Japanese had retreated from Pien Ma. (General Stillwell was cutting their supply line.)

And autumn brought furlough for the Kuhn family. We had served seven years since our last one, and now came the glad news that little daughter had been repatriated on the *Gripsholm*. Old friends of our youth (and incidentally treasurer of the CIM in North America), Mr. and Mrs. George Sutherland had taken Kathryn into their home as if she were their own child, but of course she was longing to see us. We waited only until RSBS was over, as Charles could not conduct such a big school all by himself.

As we started the long trek home to America, we had several days of truck travel first, and this gave time to think back over the two years just concluded. Two years since Eva, John, and I had come into the canyon, front fringe of battle line. It was only as I thought back over those two years that I suddenly saw it as a platform. In mind I watched the line of battle swing back and forth over Pien Ma Pass so close to us, and then I suddenly realized that constantly beset with danger and harassments we had not only been enabled to carry on our full normal schedule *but even to see advance*.

In 1942 we began a Bible school for girls.

In 1943 we began a Bible school for boys.

In 1943 and '44 we began children's work, of which I have not felt led to tell you. Eva was the stimulus, although I had had it in mind for a long time. As soon as she could speak a bit of Lisu she gathered the children of Oak Flat Village together for a Bible club every day or evening. Then we emphasized Bible, illustrated Bible, and taught Bible at the Girls' Bible School and the RSBS urging them to begin Sunday schools or Bible clubs in their villages.

As I sat back in the rattling old truck and reviewed all this, I suddenly saw the harassments as a connected series, a platform on which *the power of the Lord was manifested. That I might know Him.* Yes, we had learned much more of Him as a Helper in the challenge of small daily trials.

The scary rumors of alien soldiers approaching.

Bad weather on assembling day.

A wicked and evil magistrate interrupting and requiring to be entertained, hampering our preparations for the classroom.

An undependable goatherd and a billy called *Hitler.*

Sickness of a fellow worker.

Shortness of staff and nonarrival of essential supplies. Each too small and puny to form an arena picture in itself, but each like a tiny finger clutching at our coattails to drag us back from victory.

The challenge of the platform of small harassments in the arena—what is it? It is really the gladitorial struggle with self-pity, a most unglamorous opponent: so unglamorous that he whispers to us, "I am not important! Just let me be." How many times we have lost the fight just because we *have* let self-pity *be!*

I am reminded of a lesson not only preached but *lived* by Mrs. Alice McFarlane, principal of the CIM language school in Yangchow, Ku. She was a warrior-saint who was especially successful in downing that gladiator *Self-pity*. This is the way Mrs. McFarlane would flourish her sword at that fellow.

A rumor of approaching danger? Find out what God wants you to do, then deliberately put the *wind-words* aside. *Press on with your job!*

Bad weather when your students need dry trails to travel? Take your stand against the power of the air (Eph. 6:12-18) in prayer; claim the victory of Calvary over Satan (Heb. 2:14) then *press on* in preparation for the school, expecting victory.

Interrupting guests? Unhand the small clutching fingers of self-pity and reply to the voice that shrieks, "I can't do two things at once!" Well, take them one at a time, then.

Trust God for the ability to be gracious to the stranger within your gates, but insist that first things come first. *Press on with your job!*

That goatherd's laziness and the mess Hitler made in the storeroom? Do not let this small thing grow until it fills your thoughts. The Lord should fill your horizon always—nothing else is worthy. Clean up the mess in the storeroom or be content to leave it until you have time. But *press on with your spiritual work.*

Sickness has come down upon us and we stagger with weakness? Well, *light your lantern.* Ask Him for a promise and *press on.*

Promised supplies are delayed? Do the best you can, and refuse to pity yourself. *Press on.*

As we do this, there may come no special vision; no special miracle of deliverance; no special intervention of Providence. But after the whole experience is over you will look back, as we did, and you will be amazed at the way you have been carried along by a Power not your own. The time will come when you will stand, look back, and gasp, "How mightily was the hand of our God with us, yet we knew it not!"

Sitting there in the old truck, I reviewed our long series of harassments during those two war years, and the thing that stood out most, fairly towered above all else, was the *goodness of the Lord* in helping me. And in my heart I whispered to Him old love-words, written first of a pure human love, but, oh, so much more applicable to the perfect Love. *"Lord, I love Thee to the level of every day's most quiet need."*[4]

That is the platform of small harassments. God meets us on that level—*every day's most quiet need.* He will have a new word, a new sweetness or a new fellowship to help us press through to victory. And when the thrill of victory dawns upon us, we will whisper, "O Lord, it wasn't in me. It was Thy sufficiency for every day's most quiet need."

We adore Thee
Fall before Thee.

---

[4]Elizabeth Barrett Browning's sonnet "How Do I Love Thee?"

CHAPTER EIGHT

TAUT NERVES

THE ONLY WAY to get out of China was to fly The Hump over to India. (It was then we discovered that this famous flight went right over our part of Lisuland! Looking down, John even saw the little ferry boat at Place-of-Action.)

Into the heat and refugee crowds of India we came. World War II was still in full operation (October, 1944) and there was no passenger ship service to America. With all other civilians wishing to go home, we had to be lumped together as refugees and take what transportation the harassed authorities could provide. After some days in Calcutta and about three weeks in Bombay, we were given transportation on a troop ship going to America. Our route and port of arrival were kept secret. (Even when we landed we did not know where we were until hotel placards and street signs gave us the clue!)

So on board we went. John was sent down into the hold with the civilian men and allowed up to see us for only two hours a day. Danny and I found ourselves in an officer's cabin with other women—eleven of us, bunks three tiers high, no portholes for air, and the ship's movie theater just outside our door. They had two sittings of talkies every night so the jazz music and noise went on until nearly midnight.

Shortly after boarding. we mothers were summoned before a ship's officer for a lecture. He had probably been ordered to put fear into us, for he certainly tried his best. He told us that we were allowed on board only out of charity. This was not a passenger ship and there was no accommodation for babies. There was no baby food on board so we need not ask for it. There was no deck on the whole ship which was safe for babies—some had no railings and all had big uncovered hawseholes through which a child could easily fall. "If your child falls overboard, the ship will not stop to pick it up. I tell you now, so you need not ask! It is up to each mother to watch her own child," he shouted at us. There was no laundry room for us; just the usual washbowls. We were to eat at officers' mess but that compelled two sittings, so that each meal must be finished within half an hour. We must line up ahead of time so as not to lose a minute in getting seated. And so on. When he finished there was not one of us who would have dared to ask a favor, which was probably his purpose.

Danny was about fifteen months old, just at the toddling stage, and the trip lasted more than a month—thirty-six days, I think. Waiting in line for meals three time a day, I had to carry him, heavy as he was. To set an active toddler down meant jerking him back into line all the time, just as fatiguing as holding him. He was served a plate of officers' food—big steaks and French fried potatoes, etc. It was inevitable that his tummy would get upset, and more than one night I sat rocking him lest his cries keep the others in the cabin awake. In the daytime he had to be watched every minute lest he toddle near those yawning hawseholes. To keep him within sight while I washed his diapers was another problem. After two weeks of this I felt I was going to collapse. I remember standing in line for dinner, feeling my head beginning to swim and faintness coming over me. Again I cried out in my heart, "Lord, what can I do? Just stand till I drop?" Now the Lord could have come and touched me as He had done in the Chicago restaurant nineteen years before. But He did not choose to do so this time.

A voice called at my elbow, "Well, now, look at our poor mother carrying this big heavy boy and me doing nothing! Here, Mother, give me this young redhead!" Two strong, friendly hands removed Danny from my aching arms. It was a missionary lady from our cabin—the Lord bless her!

"Don't know why I didn't think of this before," she scolded herself. "Mother, from now on I'm self-appointed nurse for Danny. Before every meal I'm going to come and get him, wash him up, and carry him in. And after the meal I'll carry him out. Do you hear?"

Did I hear! She was an angel sent from Heaven, as far as I was concerned. And she kept her word. To me this was as much a manifestation of Christ's power as my earlier experiences. She was my "door of escape" (I Cor. 10:13, Way's Translation). God had used a natural means to deliver me, that is all.

The thirty-sixth day arrived at last: our big ship was steaming up the coast of America (we still did not know if it was the Atlantic or Pacific coast except by guesses). Rumors that we were soon to land were passed from mouth to mouth and war changes in the travel habits of America were discussed.

"They say you cannot get a taxicab any more," said one.

"And none of your friends are allowed to meet the boat," said another. This alarmed me. Our money was limited; we would need to contact our Mission soon after arrival.

"What shall we do?" I asked. Miss Alice Wishart, of Kashmir, was walking with me at the moment.

"Oh, the Lord will have something waiting for us," she replied easily. "He hasn't brought us all this way to desert us now."

And it was so. We were hours and hours getting through immigration and customs. But the Red Cross met us, provided a nurse who took Danny and cared for him—fed him, put him to bed, and watched him. Hot coffee and doughnuts were served us. We landed at ten in the morning, but it was dark before we were ready to proceed on our way. A businessman (Red Cross helper) drove us in his car from San Pedro to Los Angeles right to the door of the China Inland Mission there! I have never forgotten it. And those carefree words of Miss Wishart were to echo again and again in my heart, through many a difficult turn in life's corners in later years. "Oh, God will have something waiting for us."

It is scriptural. Psalm 59:10 (A.S.V.): "My God with his loving-kindness will meet me"; and another version translates it, "The God whose love meets me on the way."

* * *

Among our own (the bosom of the Mission Family is a wonderful place), we immediately wanted to long-distance telephone our dear girlie, Kathryn, that we had arrived. Over the wires my voice did not sound familiar to her, and it brought the tears;

but at least she had the joy of knowing we were on the same continent as she was, and would soon be speeding to her at Philadelphia. We delayed in Los Angeles only long enough to do some shopping. I was still wearing a discarded coat and beret, and so was glad we had arrived in the dark! (Just here I might digress to invite a smile. Miss Wishart met us unexpectedly in church one Sunday after our shopping expedition, and she was about to introduce me to a friend. "This is Mrs. Kuhn," she began, then noticed my new coat and hat and started to chuckle. "Mrs. Kuhn as she is, not as she was!" with laughter, to her friend's complete mystification!)

On the cross-country train ride, Danny cried every night, keeping everyone in the car awake. Nothing we could do pacified him. This was one of the most humiliating experiences of my life—and it did not help *taut nerves*.

Mr. Sutherland had thoughfully arranged for us to meet Kathryn alone in a little room. Our dear little girlie, whom we had last seen at seven and a half years of age, was now thirteen and almost at full stature. We had tried to get to her once in those intervening years, but the Japanese had bombed a bridge on our only road, so we had to turn back. But at this reunion the Lord melted us all together and there was no feeling of strangeness, praise His name!

The next six months were busy in visiting and deputation work. For the most part we stayed with our relatives, the Harrisons, who were generously hospitable, as always. Sister Kathryn's children were no longer small, however, so her home was arranged for adults. It was beautiful, with green plants in the windows but at such a low level that toddlers were tempted to reach out for the pretty trailing branches and yank them. Danny had to be watched all the time.

Everybody was wonderfully kind to me and did his best to help me rest, but at the end of six months I was as taut as on arriving. That was disappointing to everybody. How *is* a person to help such a missionary anyway? When it seems that nobody understands us, we can always turn to the Lord. Oh, it is so comforting to bury our faces in His bosom!

"Lord, I've been home for six months and I feel as ill as when I arrived. I just cannot unknot my nerves! If we only had a home of our own—owned it, so that if Danny broke or scratched anything no one else would suffer. And, oh, if I could be alone for awhile and sleep the clock around for more than one day—as many days as I needed!" What an impossible thing to ask! But quietly and gently He gave it, all of it.

John wanted to take a refresher course at Dallas Theological Seminary. None of us had ever been to Dallas, and if John was to go we must find a home there. It was war time, when houses of any kind were hard to find. The seminary had none available.

But we now discovered that we had some money! Ten years previously, John's father had died and left him some shares in a certain company. On our previous furlough the Christian manager of that firm had asked us to leave the shares there a time longer. "The company is not paying dividends now," he said, "but I firmly believe it will pay in a few years. Holding your shares and giving me your proxy will just give me a majority vote. I like to conduct this business on Christian lines and I appreciate that majority vote. So if you will hold your shares as they are, it will do me a favor." We were delighted to do so—and almost forgot we possesed any shares. Now when we made inquiry, to our astonishment we learned their value had tripled! The Christian manager had retired and was now indifferent as to whether we sold the shares or not. If we had sold in 1936 we would have received $2,000.00. By accommodating that Christian manager, we now received $6,000.00! It took our breath away—the Lord pays high interest!

Now there was hope of a place of our own at Dallas. We wrote the seminary for the names and addresses of real estate men and then wrote them our requirements. (1) It must come within our price range of less than $5,000.00. (We had to reserve something for furniture.) (2) We must be able to get possession of the house by July 28.

Then to the Lord we had requests. (1) Since we had no car, can the house be near enough to the seminary so John can walk? (2) And it should be near to a high school, so Kathryn can walk. (3) It should have two bedrooms. (4) And a fenced-in back yard where Danny can be left to play.

With the exception of one, all the real estate offices replied that a place of *any* description without *any* stipulations was *impossible,* especially in the low-price bracket! House-building materials had been requisitioned for war purposes, and so many newly married couples in the armed forces were looking for cheap homes that any available ones were snapped up before real estate offices had a chance to list them.

The one exception wrote like the others, but added that there might be a house such as we wanted available later on—the owner had not decided whether to sell or not. We wrote back to hold it for us if it was offered for sale.

About the time I had reached my extremity of nerves that would not relax, about the time of my prayer, another letter came from the real estate office in Dallas. "If one of you came immediately the owner might be persuaded to sell," they wrote, since we offered cash down, but they could not actually promise he would.

John and I went into counsel. I asked to be the one to go. We knew no one in Dallas. I would go to the YWCA and here was my chance to go to bed at seven without anyone thinking me unsociable, and without any baby-twitters at half-past five the next morning announcing that *he* (bless him!) was beginning the new day with energy. I could shop for furniture in the daytime. John was quite happy to stay behind with the children as it would give him another month with relatives and friends in his home town. Kathryn was thirteen years old and could take care of Danny—she had prayed for a baby brother! And it was summer vacation.

I had written or wired the YWCA for a room some time before, so off I went on this great adventure, my first trip to Texas. I had a good chance to witness to a young girl on the train, and walked into the YWCA in Dallas quite confident that the Lord was with me.

But it was not to be too easy. The YWCA secretary was very courteous but almost exasperated at my innocence and ignorance. Expect to have a room at the "Y" with only a week or so's advance notice? "Why, my dear," she said, "we are booked solid for months ahead. I fear I cannot even get you a hotel room. Don't you know what the war has done to America? And as for your getting a house in Dallas— I'm sorry to discourage you, but a place of any kind *without any stipulations* is like asking for the moon. I deal with people all day long, every day in the week, just like yourself. And somebody is waiting to come in now when you go out! I don't know why people cannot be told that there are no vacant houses in Dallas. Well, I will telephone and see if I can get you a room somewhere. I have already phoned nine hotels this morning and not one of them has a corner. But you are planning to stay awhile. How long did you say? A month? Well, we will see."

And then she began to phone. Inside I was praying. The first two or three places were full up. Then she tried another. "Yes," she said into the phone, "she intends to stay a month. You have a room? Oh, good. She will be right over."

"Well, you are fortunate, Mrs. Kuhn," said the secretary, hanging up the telephone. "It is a hotel in rather a bad part of town so I do not call on it often. It is quite a safe place itself but the neighborhood—well, you won't plan to roam the streets at night, I take it." I assured her I would not and she gave me the address.

It was a cheap hotel, but after Chinese inns I had learned to appreciate what America might rate third class. I had a corner bedroom with a window on each side which gave a cross-draft. It was June and the days were hot. I shared a bathroom with one other person and there were good locks on all doors. A bed, bureau, desk, and chair—what else did I need? I knelt down and thanked the Lord.

It was about noon, so I got the address of the

real estate company and proceeded downstairs. The registry clerk was a woman and very pleasant.

"Oh, your real estate office is just a couple of blocks away, and since we are right downtown, restaurants are plentiful. Woolworth has a good lunch counter too, and it is only two blocks away."

So I started out in Dallas. After a sandwich and coffee at Woolworth I was ready for *real estate*. I was perfectly sure God was going to get us that house! But how He was to do it would just be a thrilling adventure. With this confidence I made myself known to the real estate people. A sandy-haired, middle-aged salesman was put in charge of me.

"You are very lucky, Mrs. Kuhn," he said. "To get any kind of a low-priced place in Dallas, even without stipulations of any kind, is almost impossible. Of course you haven't got this place yet! But it answers your desires perfectly. It is a five-room cottage with a screened-in back porch; it is within walking distance of the seminary and also of a high school. It has a fenced-in back yard and is only half a block from the grocery and meat markets. And I think you can buy it for $4,500.00. The one snag is your stipulation that you get possession by July 28. The present owner has bought another place where he wishes to combine his business and home under the one roof, but he cannot get possession of it that soon, I fear. I will take you out there now, however, and we will talk with them."

You can imagine how eager I felt as we drove up to 1718 Ripley Street.

"Hm. It needs paint. John won't like its present appearance!" I thought to myself. But it was in a surprisingly quiet neighborhood. Across the street was a small park. And the next-door houses were not too close. It had a long, covered front porch, with a baby-gate already in!

The owners were Christians and easy to talk to. I explained our purpose in coming to Dallas, and added that if we could not get possession when we needed it, it would be useless to buy.

"Well," the owners said, "we might go and live with our daughter for a month or so. We will give you an answer tomorrow."

The third day after I arrived in Dallas the cottage was ours, money paid, deed signed, and it stipulated possession by July 28! I felt I must go and tell the YWCA secretary.

"I just thought I'd like to tell you, Mrs. ———," I said, "that I have a cottage already, bought and paid for. It meets all the stipulations and conforms to all we had wanted in addition."

She fell back in her chair and went limp, staring at me. Then as my truthfulness penetrated her understanding she sat up straight and gasped, "Mrs. Kuhn, you renew my faith in God." It had renewed mine too. That is the outcome of all God's platforms.

The platform of taut nerves. He allowed them to stretch and stretch and stretch—but not to snap. And when the time came that He said, "Enough," He had planned this lovely thing for us. "*Now no chastening for the present seemeth to be joyous, but grievous:* NEVERTHELESS AFTERWARD . . ."

God's afterwards: if they are so delightful on earth what will the *afterward* in Heaven be?

No millionaire furnishing his mansion had half the fun I did furnishing my cottage! Of course most things I had to buy second-hand. I procured a map of Dallas from the real estate office, purchased the

early morning newspaper, looked up advertisements
of second-hand things; noted what I wanted, and
started off in pursuit! I had no responsibilities, no
time schedule to hurry me, no baby depending on
my quick return, no pressure of any kind. I had
asked the Lord for a piano, an icebox, and an elec-
tric washing machine in addition to necessities—
and He gave them all. Long nights of uninterrupted
sleep renewed me. By the time three weeks had
passed I was longing for my family to come. And,
oh, the joyous day when I welcomed them to the
cottage which God had so wonderfully given us!

Of Dallas days, being together in our own wee
place was the outstanding joy. Next to that, for me,
were the young people from the seminary who began to come to us. It began with John handing
me an invitation one day to *Students' Wives Prayer
Meeting*. "You are a student's wife now," he said
with a grin. So I gladly went.

Of course I was the only middle-aged person
present! And the bevy of lovely young womanhood
that gathered for prayer simply thrilled me. Many
were earning money to put their husbands through
seminary; others were young mothers and home
keepers. All were the Lord's children and eager
to have His best for themselves and their beloved
partners. We took turns in leading with a short message and it was a joy to hear them pass on blessings
from His Word. I especially enjoyed the fact that
I was received at first as only another unit in the
group. But the fateful evening came when a new-
comer recognized me as the author of *Precious
Things of the Lasting Hills*,[1] and I was hauled out

---

[1] Out of print.

of my prized obscurity and put on the inevitable pedestal of *an author*.

How I did love those girls! Even their cultural charm meant something to me. I really had to laugh at myself—I so enjoyed their beauty, their grace of movement, the refined good taste in their dress and so on. The primitive tribes, of course, although they develop spiritually and mentally, are still crude and uncouth in their social habits.

Something within me had long been starved for the refined beauty of my own kind, such as these girls showed with every movement, and I drank it all in eagerly.

Knowing the wives led to knowing the husbands. And often vice versa, as John brought in fellow students for a chat or a cup of tea and then I found out who the wife was! In but a short time after seminary began, we were having a small group come to our home every Friday night for Bible study and prayer. As I look back on them now, *every single couple of that group reached the foreign field.* Italy, Switzerland, Formosa, China, the border of Nepal, the border of Afghanistan have felt the touch of Christ through those lives! That was a real gift from God which has permanently enriched us.

John had expected a full year at Dallas Theological Seminary. But the atom bomb changed many plans. The war ended, the State Department began to issue passports to China once more. The country was still too torn up for women and children to return safely, but the China Inland Mission sent out a letter asking the superintendents to go back to China one year ahead of their families. So we had to face it. From the beginning, the motto of our married life has been *God first,* and every now

and again we are challenged with it anew. It is our
joy to reproclaim it, so this time there was no argument. The Lord gave us II Corinthians 4:12: *"So
then death worketh in us, but life in you."* We felt
it meant death in the sense of breaking up our
family life, that the Lisu might gain spiritually.

So John sailed for China in January, 1946.

I was grateful for the extra year with Kathryn.
This is a discussion of *platforms,* not really a record
of family life. But I was continually grateful for the
way God had fathered and mothered her in the years
we had been forced apart, and very grateful for
her loving companionship and help in the almost
two years we were together.

When it came to leaving Dallas, the Lord again
worked wonderfully. I wanted to sell the house as
it stood, furniture and all. One day an elderly married couple knocked at our door. They had heard
we were thinking to sell and asked how much I
wanted. I said $6,100.00 and they paid the full
amount in cash. So the Lord had given us a home
of our own, practically rent-free and money enough
to pay our way back to Pennsylvania! The taut
nerves were relaxed by the time the return to China
had come.

The platform of taut nerves is not without its
own kind of suffering. It may be He has to allow
us to get so desperate that we will be willing to attempt the impossible with Him, before He sends
us relaxation. Whatever the reason for His allowing those circumstances it is also a place where
His fellowship is found. It is a place where His
power will be manifested. And the end of it is that
we know Him better. *You renew my faith in God*
will be the testimony of onlookers.

Shadows and shine art Thou,
  Dear Lord, to me;
Pillar of cloud and fire,
  I follow Thee.
What though the way is long,
In Thee my heart is strong,
Thou art my joy, my song—
  Praise, praise to Thee.
                    —Amy Carmichael

CHAPTER NINE

SEEMING DEFEAT

Back to China on a slow, small freighter we traveled, Danny and I. Kathryn we left in Philadelphia with the dear Sutherlands.

"Promise me not to cry, sister!" shouted the small three-year-old brother, alarmed at her tearful face as the train pulled out of the station. "Promise me not to cry!"

We sailed from Houston; there had been a longshoremen's strike and ships were still scarce, so we had no choice. The *Joseph Lee* had no railings and took forty-six days to make the passage! Miss Ruth Nowack of our Mission traveled with us, and the only other passengers were a young mother and two children. Mrs. Dorothy Greenwood was going to join her aviator husband in Shanghai. Our cargo was kerosene and cotton! Some of the crew wanted to back out when they heard it; but this was one reason the old boilers were not pushed very hard, making our passage leisurely.

Ruth was a great blessing to all of us. She proved an enchanting storyteller to the children, and was so unselfish in helping us mothers. We began to have Sunday school, and Mrs. Greenwood asked if we could not have it every day. We did, and had Bible study with her—none of us realizing how God had tenderly arranged that she might learn to know Him before impending tragedy struck her.

The day before we landed, the door of my cabin was thrown open and in dashed beautiful Dorothy Greenwood screaming and weeping.

She had just heard over her radio that her husband had been killed when his airplane crashed on Christmas day. It was our sad privilege to care for her.

I had expected John to meet us at the Shanghai wharf, but he had been delayed; so Danny and I, arriving in the big CIM compound in bitter cold weather, had to wait. John had been touring the province of Yunnan in a survey of the tribes and had not been able to get back to civilization when he had hoped. Lucius was with him.

Jim Greenwood's crash was followed by a similar catastrophe in which Mrs. Meller of the CIM and her three children were killed. Little Peter Meller had been playing with Danny only the day before, so it brought it acutely home to us. In both cases the fault was not the pilots,' but the careless preparation of the plane. Generalissimo Chiang ordered all planes grounded for an investigation, and our wait in Shanghai was prolonged.

The bridges which had been blown up by the Japanese were still not repaired, so transportation into the far interior was a real problem. When John finally did arrive, the matter was discussed carefully. It was decided that John and Eric Cox drive the baggage of several families (Kuhns' included) in a truck and that Danny and I go by air. The men would have to drive across China, with broken roads, half-mended bridges, and other dangers. It would be too hard a trip for a woman and child. Eventually Danny and I obtained space in an army freighter, a Flying Fortress, and it was wonderful to arrive in balmy Yunnan after the bleak cold of Shanghai.

In Kunming we had to wait for John and the truck, but while there we had a memorable reunion with Lucius. Eva I had left in Tali with Mrs. Dr. Watson. When the Watsons left for furlough, Eva entered Tali Hospital to train as a nurse. We would see her as we passed through.

In returning to China this time the one thing I had feared was travel on the Burma Road. Yet that term the only time I had to make a long trip on it was with my dear husband as driver! From Kunming to Paoshan we rode on the truck, and for the first and only time I thoroughly enjoyed the Burma Road. I once heard Mrs. Ruth Stull say that the dangers she had feared when she went to South America never met her, but dangers far worse awaited her! I had to smile, remembering my last term in China when this had happened also to me. So it does no good to imagine the evils that await us! And for the unimagined ones the Lord is sufficient, so let us be at peace.

At Tali we met Eva. She pleaded with tears to be allowed to go back to Lisuland with us.

"But, my dear," I reasoned, "you have only a year and a half left and you will graduate! If you leave now you get no credit whatever."

"I don't care about credits or certificates," she cried. "I am happy just to be with you and Ma-pa and Danny." If it had not been for my stern lessons in 1942 about inordinate affections, I would have been tempted to take her with us. I would sorely need help such as hers in the days ahead. But those lessons had left scars which protected Eva from my possessiveness, and though she did not see it then, I am sure she has been grateful many times since. Our dear little Eva—she is behind the Bamboo Curtain now and we never hear of her. The last word was that she was trying to get permission to study to be a doctor—so I am sure she understands now why we let her cry in 1947!

Failing to get permission to give up her nursing, Eva asked for her annual leave in order to be with us on the trip to Paoshan. Nurse Irene Neville did the same, so we had them in the truck on the next lap of the journey. And we needed them. Climbing a steep hairpin-turn ascent we came on a Chinese truck newly wrecked, with the injured perhaps dying, lying on the road beneath. We stopped, and our two nurses administered first aid to them.

At Paoshan the Christians received us joyfully. The China Inland Mission no longer had a house in that city, so we had all to live in the chapel, while John, as superintendent, tried to rent another place for the missionaries who were to arrive soon after us. As a matter of fact, our own relatives, Kathryn and David Harrison, were appointed to take charge of the Paoshan work. This was to include caring for young workers who, we hoped, would later go to the tribes. So a large house was needed. Such a one was in prospect and soon John was involved in all the slow bargaining of the East.

Seeing that it was going to be a long process (it actually took three months before John was released to come into Lisuland and join us), I asked my husband to let Danny and me go into Lisuland ahead of him. Eva had to return to the hospital; Lucius was chafing to get home (he had been

gone almost a year); there would then be no one
to help me supervise Danny, and only the public
chapel to live in! So it was decided that Lucius escort us back into Oak Flat. Eva and Miss Neville
traveled with us as far as Wa Yao, where the Lisu
trail enters the Burma Road. Here we said good-
by, Eva weeping rebelliously, and we began the difficult over-mountain journey.

I was surprised at the desolation of the trail. Little villages where we used to stop for lunch were
now deserted ghost hamlets. "There were too many
robbers and brigands on the main road," explained
Lucius. "The people have fled out of sight. Soldiers,
disbanded far from home, have turned bandit. It
is still dangerous."

We had Chinese coolies to carry us and our things
and they grumbled every stage. "When we get to
the Salween and meet Lisu Christians, you will be
well fed and your loads carried for you," we encouraged them, but they were openly unbelieving.

Yet it was true. The last day, at the last steep
2,000-foot climb, Lisu with horses were waiting for
us! Oh, what a loving jubilant reunion! Danny had
a horse to himself, and two Lisu, one on each side,
walked close beside to guard the delighted three-
year-old. "Mummy! My horse has bells and yours
doesn't!" he shouted in elation. "My horse rides
bumpily." The astonished Chinese had their loads
taken off their shoulders and shifted onto Lisu
backs. When, at the end of the climb a delicious
feast of pork was given to us all, one of those men
came to me, his eyes shining. "*Chen-chen, Szu-mu!
Ni shuo-ti pu-ts'o!*" ("It is true after all, Lady, what
you said!") . . . We tried to witness to him of the
change Jesus Christ works in human lives.

The welcome party over, we settled down to the grim problems of re-establishment. Lucius said good-by and departed for his own home at Village of the Olives, across the river. I will quote from our circular.

The poor old shanty (now twelve years old) was a dilapidated sight—it leaned toward the precipice very distinctly and its thatched roof had been blown off in great patches. Inside, the furniture looked rougher than even memory could recall, and everything was covered with the rust and debris of nine months' vacancy. But Ruth (Pade-John's wife; they were the caretakers) had swept the floor and had prepared lots of cold drinking water and hot water for baths! Now none of you in luxurious America can appreciate what that last meant. I record it for the benefit of the angels (and fellow missionaries) who saw our rough journey in. (The third night we slept in a hayloft, and the fourth in a deserted corn bin, and the fifth we were nearly eaten up with fleas.) So we appreciated our welcome. It was a rainy day, but the Lord mercifully held the rain off just those two hours when we had to climb—it came down wet and plenty as soon as we were in the house. That did not seem like a nice welcome, but we learned gradually that that was the *first rain for half a year*—everybody had been praying for it for months. It rained for the next two days, a token from God to the church that His blessing is connected with the reception of His messengers and His Gospel.

This token was needed, for the church as a whole had been letting down the boundaries of separation from the world, and this is always followed by coldness toward God. The saddest news was of the backsliders of this village where we live. The robbers who broke into our house last December were the old thief, as expected, but with him were two of our former church leaders. Knowing us so well one of them knew just where our valuables were usually kept, making it easy for them to help themselves. Christ had a Judas among His closest ones, and now we know a bit of how that hurts. But all in the village are not so. As they crowded in to see me day by day, many a little tale of poverty and suffering, and a warm hand-squeeze of gratitude that once more we have come to help them, made me praise God for the privilege of being here again.

They have indeed suffered. Their clothing is ragged and the dearth of rain killed vegetables and such. They brought love-offerings as Lisu have always done, but they were almost all eggs, as there was nothing else to bring. Corn from last year's harvest fed the chickens. Over a hundred eggs were given us in just a few days. Sunday they came thronging from all over the mountain—some three hundred of them—to church. How they enjoyed the new phonograph and the "Hallelujah Chorus" record and Fuller's quartette records and others I had brought! Every day I am requested to play it. And how they shrieked with joy over Kathryn's baby doll which I had brought back (a cast-off doll, but it shuts its eyes and cries when you lay it down). But the biggest miracle of all to them is Danny's mechanical train which rings a bell and spouts fire from its chimney. I am afraid it will be worn out before Christmas, it is so much in demand.

All in all, it was a happy return to a needy field. In the medical line alone the need is pitiful. At Six Treasuries they swarmed us with requests for medicine—said that there had been none brought into the canyon for many months, and the obvious need of medicine is seen everywhere among the people. Pray for us that we may fulfill His purposes in this place. Thieves are plentiful over the whole district—they say the new laird nourished them. Pray that we may be enabled to work in peace.

PRAYER OF REDEDICATION

Take charge afresh, dear Holy Spirit, as Thou didst seven years ago, and may my assurance not necessarily be in the great joy of those days but . . . from Thy words, "Thou shalt receive power when the Holy Ghost shall come upon thee." Power . . . to keep my heart warm and at rest when coldness and disappointments crowd around; power to steady my faith when the enemy of souls seems everywhere to be making terrific headway; power to see the hand of God quietly and persistently at work.—ANON.

Among church leaders of Oak Flat Village who were a disappointment were Pade-John and Keh-deh-seh-pa.

Pade-John had once been a wonderful Christian. He had given free the land on which our house stood! So he was the natural person to be caretaker during our absence on furlough. The change in him had come after his marriage to a nominal Christian named Ruth. Ruth was pretty and came of an influential family but was utterly unprincipled. We could not lay our finger on anything, but from the first I instinctively distrusted her. I wanted to get Pade-John to break off the engagement; which rather scandalized him as he was not aware of her true character and would not believe it. But after eleven years of marriage to her, laziness, shady ways of getting money, immoral talk and laughter in the home had turned him into a hypocrite. Both of them being clever, they covered up their tracks so well that no one could get proof of what we all suspected.

Keh-deh-seh-pa had become political headman of the village of Oak Flat after Me-do-me-pa died. He had seen the power that good man received from the Holy Spirit and, like Simon Magus, coveted it. He tried very hard to become head deacon in the church, but spiritual power cannot be imitated. He was feared but not trusted.

The old thief over the hill never had been a Christian, and he had robbed us before. But the whole countryside was filled with robbers. I had been told that there were sixty of them operating within a small radius of us, and three times at night they tried to attack us. Danny and I were the only ones sleeping in the shanty, and at first I left the bedroom windows open all night as had always been my custom. Then one night (the first attempt) I was awakened by a bird call, clear and powerful, right beneath that open window. One spring, and an active fellow could be over the sill and into our room! I knew it was not a bird at that time of night, and then I heard an answering call from behind our house. I went cold all over, and could do nothing but lie there and pray. Again this one called and that one answered. I would have been comforted if only I had known that Mr. Yang, Pade-John, and Joel were up and stalking them! The calls meant, "It's all up. They're after us. Let's run." Not knowing that, I lay there petrified. It was not lack of faith that the Lord could keep me! I knew that. It was not unwillingness to suffer. It was just suspense. God does allow missionaries to be killed, now and again. Would this be that?

The next morning I sent for some of the Christian men whom I knew I could trust and told them of my scare. From that day on, one of them slept in our house with a gun each night until husband John arrived. Although Oak Flat Village had its backsliders, there were dear loyal saints around too.

When Lucius heard of our insecurity, he wrote inviting us to move our home to Village of the Olives where he lived and where he could protect me while John was away on these long trips as superintendent. But I would not consider it. The two things that white people require such a lot of were very hard to obtain at Olives—water and fuel. Olives had only one water hole and the girls often got up at three or four in the morning in order to get water for the family breakfast! All the trees near Olives had been cut down for firewood—the villagers had to go a long way to get any. And the Kuhn family, with their western ideas of frequent laundry, used a lot of both water and firewood. At Oak Flat were the Bible school dormitory buildings which had been built up during these years. I did not see how we could possibly move our station, and did not give it serious thought. *I did not even pray about it.*

John arrived from Paoshan before the Rainy Season Bible School, and that summer (1947) we had a record number of students and had to use the Chinese schoolhouse to accommodate them. I tried to teach children's work to the evangelists. There were no such things as Sunday schools, for instance, except what Eva had begun in Oak Flat Village, and Lucius had started one in Village of the Olives. Our RSBS students carried their vision back to the villages at the end of the summer. Said one

Christian woman to Jeremiah, "When the young folks came back from RSBS and gave their testimonies, I was so thrilled that I could not sleep all that night until cock-crow, for thinking of what they had said."

The rainy season passed, and John had to go out on another trip. He had no sooner gone than Danny came down with typhus fever and I was left alone to nurse him! During this time and for several more months I was the only white missionary for many days' journey in the canyon, and the church leaders brought all problems to me.

The work at Oak Flat became more and more disappointing. Caught in flagrant sin, Keh-deh-seh-pa had to be put out of office as deacon, for the Lisu church practices New Testament discipline—and he was not pleased about it.

Those in the village itself who stood with me for righteousness were slowly but steadily melting away. Mrs. Yang developed tuberculosis, and her husband had to take her back to Chinaland where the food was more what she required. This not only deprived me of a Christian man in the village who would back me up, but it left the position of teacher in the Chinese school vacant. Immediately Keh-deh-seh-pa applied for the position in the name of his second son who had been studying Chinese at Tali. The boy was a profligate—Eva had heard of his dissolute doings and told me. But the one-time Strong Man of our village, Me-do-me-pa, was now dead. To my horror the other deacons were afraid to say no—Keh-deh-seh-pa was rich and had political power! My Irish spunk arose (alas, it is always ready to push me into impetuous action!), so I said *no*, flatly, and the deacons eagerly shel-

tered behind Ma-ma! If Lucius had been there, or
some of our fine deacons farther north, they would
have led in that responsibility.

Then came a night when Keh-deh-seh-pa and his
rejected son, under cover of darkness and knowing
I was alone in the shanty, entered the house to
threaten me. You see, I had no absolute proof of the
son's sin. But God, who has mercy on His impetuous
Peters, caused a poor Christian farmer to see the
two sneaking through the dark; he followed them
and a few minutes after their entrance (when I was
petrified with fright) I saw dear Chu-fu-si-pa slip
in and take a chair in the corner. He pretended he
wanted to sell me some charcoal. This provided
a witness to our conversation, and as they tried to
trick me into statements which could be used in a
lawsuit against me, the Lord gave me the answers.
I knew it was the right answer when Chu-fu-si-pa
would silently beam on me. Their plot failed, and
a fine Christian Lisu who spoke Chinese was given
the position of schoolmaster.

But from then on a subtle persecution set in—
accidents happened to our goatherd; our water supply was taken from us and we had to go to another
faraway, inconvenient one. Life in Oak Flat Village
for a woman alone was getting dangerous. John
was gone for months: five months one year, seven
months another year. When my continuance in this
way seemed impossible, Charles Peterson arrived
back from furlough!

God was trying to uproot me, but He kept His
promise of I Corinthians 10:13: "There hath no temptation taken you but such as is common to man:
but God is faithful, who will not suffer you to be
tempted above that ye are able; but will with the

temptation also make a way to escape, that ye may be able to bear it." He never let me suffer more than I could bear.

The climax came at the end of the 1948 Rainy Season Bible School. Pade-John had asked to attend that school. I was more and more doubtful of him and Ruth; they did not ring true. But I never dreamed of what they would attempt. Pade-John had been away from home that spring, and while he was gone I noticed his wife Ruth going into the bedroom of our cookboy, Jana. I ordered her off the premises (she and Pade-John lived just below us on the hill). But it was whispered about the village that she and Jana had sinned. Neither would admit it, but they were suspended from Communion.

Rainy Season Bible School of 1948 saw another splendid body of students gather. A group came from Burma! One of whom had walked seventeen days in order to be present. Several came from the Mid-Salween area—a rather recent development of the work.

At the end of the school, it was the custom for each student to write the staff a letter, telling what they hoped to do for the Lord during the next year. To our concern, Pade-John wrote us that he was applying for the pastorate of the Mid-Salween work! Of course he got *no* for a reply. With a wife such as he had, how could a pastorate be given him? In any case we did not feel that he himself was fit for it, although he had done well as a student. But I had learned now (John had known it long before, of course) that it was dangerous to make a charge against anyone without absolute proof in black and white. It is difficult to find this kind of evidence for unspirituality. But to our surprise, Pade-John refused to admit defeat and began making preparations to go!

It was the last day of RSBS when crowds from all the surrounding villages had gathered for the closing exercises. The program had no sooner finished than Keh-deh-seh-pa appeared with Pade-John, a large rabble of local farmers carrying clubs and, in the midst of them, Jana and Ruth roped like criminals.

"Here is where they sinned and here is where I'll have them beaten!" called out Keh-deh-seh-pa, triumphantly.

Little Danny was playing at the side of our shanty. I quickly ran to him, called a friend aside and asked her to take Danny for a walk into the ravine. Lisu beatings are brutal, and I did not want the little five-year-old to witness one. With Danny out of the way, I sped back to the shanty. Lucius met me with a face like a thundercloud.

"Don't go into your kitchen, Ma-ma," he whispered. "They have tied Jana to one wall of it and Ruth to the other. Keh-deh-seh-pa has used his civil authority as the village magistrate, and anyone who unties them will be taken to Chinese law. He says they sinned there and they will be tied there until Ma-pa signs a paper giving the Mid-Salween pastorate to Pade-John!"

"But he cannot do that!" I said indignantly. "They did not sin there! Look how tiny the kitchen is. Besides, it is the kitchen of Americans!"

Lucius looked dubious. "Better go slow, Ma-ma," he counseled. "Interference with the carrying out of Chinese justice might be an ugly accusation in the hands of an unprincipled man like Keh-deh-seh-pa. Ma-pa is trying to reason with him. Better just pray about it." Lucius was as indignant as I was, but much more accustomed to the wily tricks of so-called justice in the canyon. So I tried to pray.

Hours passed. Danny was brought back and clamored for his supper. I had no cook now and no Eva. I had to go into the kitchen and prepare our meal. I wonder if you can imagine my feelings, trying to do that with a living human being bound to the left wall and another bound to the right wall! I made tea first and offered it to the prisoners. Jana refused. He was ashamed and savage with anger. Keh-deh-seh-pa had committed adultery only a few months before and no one had bound *him* and dragged *him* through the village! Ruth was brazen. Their hands being tied behind them I had to hold the cup while she drank thirstily. She would have chatted if I had allowed her to! So I prepared supper, helped by Mrs. Estella Kirkman who was our guest-speaker at that school. She had given an excellent course on children's work and she stayed with us until Christmas.

Keh-deh-seh-pa had kept John talking for hours. This was exactly what he wanted—a huge audience from all over the country and the white man begging him to relent his power and *he refusing*.

On Sundays Christians from surrounding villages came to Oak Flat for noon worship. Closing day is always on a Sunday, so the church audience also witnessed Keh-deh-seh-pa's revenge. Deacon Ah-be-pa of Plum Tree Flat sent the women and children home but he with certain stalwart young men of his village stayed to help John.

Dark fell. Keh-deh-seh-pa, Pade-John, and the rabble took themselves down the mountain to eat their dinner. The two were still tied, standing in our kitchen. Ten o'clock at night came and John ordered me to bed. Being of a sympathetic nature, the whole thing wrought on me emotionally. I went to bed but of course I could not sleep. Then I heard the rabble coming up the hill toward us. Wild shouts and loud talking rent the night. I was about to get up and dress again when Lucius' voice sounded at the door.

"May I come in, Ma-ma?"

"Yes, yes," I cried. "What has happened?"

He came in looking so dejected. He sat down in silence and just shook his head.

"What's the noise? What has happened?" I urged.

"Ah-be-pa, dear old man, decided that he would cut the prisoners loose. He said if a white man got involved in it, it might become a consular affair and spread all over the province. If he, a Lisu farmer and church official did it, it would only be judged in the canyon. So he went and cut Ruth and Jana free."

"Good. They're gone then?"

"Yes. But Ruth must have told. For Keh-deh-seh-pa's rabble got wind of it and came up the hill brandishing their clubs for revenge. They caught hold of old Ah-be-pa and you know what that would do to Caleb, Simon, and the other fellows from Plum Tree Flat who love their old deacon so! They sprang to defend him, and there was going to be a free-for-all fight when Ma-pa cried out, 'I'll sign the paper!' Then, of course, it stopped."

"Oh, he didn't!" I cried, aghast.

Lucius tried to comfort me. "He did it, committing it to God, Ma-ma. It was that, or a terrible battle; and think how the Lord would be dishonored if the heathen heard the Christians were fighting one another! For Pade-John and Keh-deh-seh-pa still call themselves Christians. The paper is not worth anything anyway. Who would have such a fellow as a pastor now? Fool that he was to do such a thing on *this day* of all days. In a week's time the students will all be back in their homes and Pade-John's Judas-trick will be known all over the land! Oh, what a fool Satan makes of his tools!" and Lucius flung his arms out wide to show the emptiness wrought.

Just then my weary husband came in. He looked at Lucius and me, then said to him, "You've told her?" He sat down and buried his face in his hands.

Defeat. How can the *power of His resurrection* be shown on such a platform? As a family we have always believed Romans 8:28: "*All things work together for good to them that love God.*" I know that modern translations change that verse so that it does not give that promise. The translation may be changed *but the fact remains*. God does work *all things* together for good to them that follow Him in loving obedience.

I dare to say "*all things*"? I dare. That will include sin—and dishonorable defeat? Yes, but do not misunderstand me. God will never *condone* sin or dishonorable defeat. Let us take sin first.

David was never the same man after his sin; a certain fearless manliness was gone forever. He vaccillated when it came to punishing his sons, and so on. *Selah.* (*Selah*, used to designate a change of instrumentation in the Psalms, has been translated . . . "*think of that.*") The punishment of his sin was not withdrawn. *Selah*.

But from the moment David cried to God, "I have

sinned," the fragments of the wreck of his noble life were gathered into God's hands and quietly wrought into another vessel. Not as beautiful as the first would have been. *Selah*. But from that moment on, for David there was hope, a future and the loving embrace of his Father's arms. A future? Some of his writings which have most helped succeeding generations were his penitential psalms. *Selah*. On the Father's bosom there is always hope. And Romans 8:28 is a fact, no matter how you translate it!

Defeat, when it is not sin but a sort of spiritual Dien-Pien-Phu, may also claim Romans 8:28. The enemy comes in overwhelming numbers and it is not a question of victory but of which is less dishonorable to the dear Lord. Or perhaps we have tried to do something for Him and it has ended in humiliating failure. Dorothy Bidlake once said to me, "Philippians 4:6, Isobel! 'Be careful for nothing'—*not even your failures*." Her words came to me that night at Oak Flat. It seemed sacrilege not to care about what had happened that Closing Day! But the word *careful* in the Old English sense does not mean *concerned*. Of course we should care about success or failure. *Careful* in the King James Version means *full of care; anxious* is how Knox translates it; *fret* is Way's translation. We are not to fret over our defeats and failure. We are to confess them, to commit them to Him, to seek the next step under His guidance and to withhold judgment on that matter until God has completed it. "Why did God ever allow this?" the flesh cries out, aghast. I know it did in me that night. Oak Flat Village, where we had labored for thirteen years—to see a scene like it witnessed that Sunday! I was leveled to the earth in humiliation. I had still to experience what our wonderful Lord can do *with defeat*.

The very first thing this did was to cause us to move. Lucius came in the next morning (he and the other students were going home). "Well, Mama," he said, "you will have to move over to the Village of the Olives. You can never stay alone in this village now—can you?"

"No, I would not dare, Lucius," I said sadly, "but what shall we do for water and fuel?"

"I've been thinking and I have a plan," he answered. "The wood will have to be carried a long way but I think we can burn charcoal for you. The water? Well, you know there is only a fight for the water at mealtimes. All night it flows, overflows the pool, runs off into the valley and is lost! Now if we got a bamboo pipe carrying the water, a night's flow would be enough, wouldn't it?"

"Yes, it would."

"Good. Then I'm going home to build you and Ma-pa a house on my ground next to Mary's and my big new one. Or you can share our new house if you like."

"No," I said quickly, "I'd like a place of my own."

"All right. We'll set to work. Ma-pa," he asked John, "when do you leave on your next trip?"

"Very soon," John replied, "but I've arranged for Mrs. Kirkman to stay on until Christmas and New Year. Betty Ju, the Chinese girl, will be here too."

"And if you get scared, Ma-ma," said our big-hearted Boy, "you can all come over and live with me *any time*. Do you understand? *Any time!*"

We thanked him and he left.

I was not thrilled at the prospect of leaving my

long, quiet bedroom at the edge of the abyss. Lucius' farm was almost in the center of the Village of the Olives—noise around you day and night. There was an unpleasant danger approaching Oak Flat of which none of us knew anything, but God knew. We moved our home from Oak Flat to Village of Olives in December, 1948. Four months later, Oak Flat Village was invaded by a band of Communist brigands! They were led by a Chinese named Dai Yi-gwan, a man who was my personal enemy. (I had found him out in oppressing the poor Lisu and had stood up for the people. It took his face away and he hated me from that day on.) He was like a demon incarnate. (*Stones of Fire,** pp. 150-152 tells how he treated the laird who was his covenant-friend, a sacred relationship in the canyon.) On their way to Oak Flat Village they inquired specially if I were there! And Keh-deh-seh-pa joined hands with Dai Yi-gwan. I shuddered to think what would have been my fate if God had not uprooted me and sent me across the Salween River just out of reach.

When I heard how his band had conquered the three lairds at Six Treasuries, the first question I asked was, "Did Dai Yi-gwan join them?"

"Yes," was the answer, "he was their leader to the laird at Place-of-Action."

I was told later that Dai Yi-gwan had plans to come across the river, when God again intervened. The story of how young laird Dwan captured his captors in one bloody night's carnage at Place-of-Action, and later had to order the death of his traitor-friend Dai Yi-gwan (best man at Laird Dwan's wedding) is told in *Stones of Fire*.

---

*Moody Press.

I heard of that death with shuddering gratitude.

Another *good thing* in our removal was that it brought us nearer to certain areas of heathen Lisu who responded to the Gospel before we were finally driven out by the communists.

And then—listen to this!—*there was not one ill-effect of that awful affair that I can remember.* The paper John signed? It was just as Lucius had prophesied. The next morning when we awoke, a letter had been thrust under our door. It was signed by the RSBS students from the Mid-Salween. It said something like this:

> Dear Pastor Kuhn,
> We are leaving before dawn so that Pade-John will not find out. We hear he planned to go back with us. We don't want such a man for our pastor! We know you were forced to sign that paper, but we are hurrying back to warn the Mid-Salween church that it was forced from you. *We won't have him.*
>
> Signed————

Pade-John did not even attempt to claim that pastorate. He was feared and abhorred everywhere he went. Finally he wrote us an apology, confessing how wrong he had been! Still no one wanted him. Finally he deserted Ruth (who, lazy and idle all her life then had to work for her living) and he went far into Burma. But you remember that summer we had had one student come seventeen days' journey to study with us. Everywhere the churches had been warned against Pade-John. The last I heard was six years later he was found digging roads in Burma for the government—but still claiming to be a Christian. Satan is a merciless master.

What of Keh-deh-seh-pa, the green bay tree (Ps. 37:35)? He never expected Dai Yi-gwan to lose and Laird Dwan to win. When that happened he fled for his life and hid in caves of the mountains. Laird Dwan moved over to Village of the Olives and one evening I overheard him next door talking to some spies he was sending across the river to hunt down Keh-deh-seh-pa. "And when you find him, *I'm going to skin him alive*," he snorted angrily. They did that in the canyon.

My heart failed me. I could not wish that for any enemy, and I started to pray that Keh-deh-seh-pa would repent so that God could deliver him. I had no faith that he would! I just prayed that way anyway. It is unbelievable what our God can do. First we heard that Keh-deh-seh-pa had bought pardon by a huge gift to the laird and many smooth protestations that he had no idea Dai Yi-gwan, the lairds' own covenant-friend, had any evil purposes in that trip, and so on and so on.

But I was totally unprepared for what happened next. My diary records that on Saturday, January 14, 1950, Keh-deh-seh-pa arrived at Village of the Olives to confess his faults to Mr. Kuhn, to ask forgiveness, to make a public apology to the whole church on Sunday and to ask to be taken back into the church! Even after having prayed for this to happen I had a hard time believing the man to be sincere. Such is the weakness of us human beings.

He was brought up before the deacon body and the two men missionaries, John, and Charles Peterson. The meeting took place in our shanty. The house at Oak Flat, which John built, was roomy; the one which the Lisu built for us at Olives had a wonderful thatch on the roof but otherwise it was small. The central room was dining room, study, medical dispensary, and guest room all in one. The deacons brought Keh-deh-seh-pa here; and Lucius, who had been typing for the church, had to pick up the typewriter and move into the next room, which was our storeroom. Kitchen, guest room, and storeroom was all the shanty contained. We slept in a loft over the storeroom. I, being a female, was never asked to meetings of the diaconate, and I had not the smallest ambition to be invited. But since they were in the central room I had to stay in the kitchen or storeroom. I did not even try to listen to their conversation, but prayed in my heart that the Lord's will be done.

After about an hour, to my astonishment, John called me in. "Keh-deh-seph-pa has made his confession to us all," he said, "but the deacons wonder if there is not something he should confess to Mama too. Would you care to question him? Have you anything against him?"

It had been a humbling process and it showed on Keh-deh-seh-pa's face. But I felt that now was the golden opportunity to deal straight with the man. John, Charles, and the deacons had probably done so but it would not hurt to put it as I saw it. So I said, "I'm just afraid, Keh-deh-seh-pa, that your desire to be reinstated in the church is only to gain a respectable cloak for your late escapades."

"What escapades, Ma-ma?" he asked simply. I named several things I had heard attributed to him.

His face lit up. "But Ma-ma, I have been maligned. It was this way"—and he proceeded to explain away his crimes, with quite obvious enjoyment. He had an amazing facility for wriggling out of situations and a smoothness of explanation that sounded most plausible. I was exasperated. We were missing the point.

"That may be so, Keh-deh-seh-pa," I said, "but my concern for you is that you have never been *born again.* I have no personal animosity for you whatever. I do not hate you, in fact, I have been praying for you. I wish no confession from you touching myself. But I would like to know your own inner state before the Lord. No amount of public confession will bring you into His kingdom, if you have never said, 'Lord, I'm a sinner and I need a Saviour.'"

He looked abashed. Then lifted his eyes to mine and said, "I believe my sins are forgiven, Ma-ma. I believe I am born again."

"Then," said I, turning to the deacons, "if the diaconate pass you for readmittance into fellowship, I will pass you too."

So saying, I left the room and went into the storeroom. Lucius, typing energetically, did not look at me, but as I passed close to him to get some potatoes, he whispered, "Strait is the gate and narrow is the way."

My mind was now on dinner and I did not get his point. To one side was a big corn bin, to another a rice bin, and then the long potato bin. Space was at a premium—did he mean that? Keh-deh-seh-pa and the diaconate were still in the next room separated only by a bamboo wall. Lucius made a gesture of impatience, beckoned me to lean closer and whispered, "*Strait is the gate.* Keh-deh-seh-pa wriggled this way, he squirmed that way; he said it was a mistake, a moment of weakness, a snare of the Devil. He wanted to call it by anything but its real name *sin*. But it is a strait gate. He had to come to it. *There is no other way in.*"

I was thrilled with the spiritual insight with which Lucius had watched the poor sinner's evasions. We looked at each other, nodding our heads, and there was the moment of that wonderful fellowship that is a joy beyond anything of earth. Both Lucius and I had entered that strait gate; we knew the simple firmness of our Lord in holding man to it; we also knew the freedom and blessing of the kingdom on the inside! If only the poor sinner will shelve his excuses, knuckle down, and *enter in!*

> So little is the door—stoop low—all else must go
> But oh, how much they win, who enter in.

And so, only one year and four months after Keh-deh-seh-pa's green bay tree triumph, he had come to apologize and confess what a failure it had been.

The platform of defeat and failure—don't fret about it. Do not quickly assume it is the end of the matter—it isn't. Wait for God to work, and believe our Lord when He says the gates of Hell shall not prevail against His kingdom.

I have often been impressed by the dramatic picture so simply disclosed in II Timothy 4—the last recorded words of Paul.

He knew his life was drawing to a close. If he had used physical sight only, he would have had to say, "My lifework has been a colossal failure." He, the saintliest of men, was in chains; he was brought thus before Nero, the vilest of men. One student of Nero's life has said of him, "He was only mud and blood." Yet Nero was on the throne, and Paul the saint a prisoner before him.

"At my first answer no man stood with me, but all men forsook me," Paul wrote later. What a disappointment! There were supposed to be stalwart saints in Rome at that time. His dear friends had deserted him. But not all. *"Notwithstanding the Lord stood with me."* Yea, there is one Friend who never fails us.

"This thou knowest, that all they which are in Asia be turned away from me" (II Tim. 1:15). Why, Asia comprised some of Paul's most cherished fruit! Years of his life had been spent to establish those young churches. And now, in the last epistle he wrote before he died, he says they had repudiated him. Doubtless his old enemies, the Judaizers, had influenced them.

What a melancholy picture! What a way to end a life of such self-sacrifice! Himself in bonds, shortly to be condemned and executed. His friends had deserted him. His spiritual children had repudiated him. Paul, your life is a colossal failure!

"Oh, no," he says quietly, using the eyes of faith. "I have fought a good fight . . . henceforth there is laid up for me a crown of righteousness." There is no defeat in those words.

And now we, nineteen centuries later, may be judges as to which saw correctly—Paul's eyes of faith, or the fleshly eye of sight? The eye of faith saw correctly.

The platform of seeming defeat and failure will conform us to His image in humility. If we wait patiently we shall some day see His power working in undreamed-of ways. And we shall *know Him; as* with Paul, *the Lord will stand by us and strengthen us.*

The foe meant thine ill,
The Father thy blessing,
Always 'tis so.
O Heart, be thou still,
However distressing
Sharp winds that blow.
           —DOHNAVUR

CHAPTER TEN

BETWEEN THE
SCISSORS' KNIVES

A<small>NY</small> C<small>HRISTIAN</small>, who finds himself betwen two
extremely dangerous situations, finds himself
held there without possibility of escape, needs guidance from the Lord. So this chapter will touch a
bit on that subject. But first, in order that the two
knives of the scissors be understood, we must explain some things.

Politically, the canyon of the Upper Salween was
governed by Chinese magistrates who worked with
local feudal lairds. These lairds owned most of the
mountains, and were a mixture of Chinese and tribes.
On the whole they were ignorant opium smokers,
and thoroughly evil. No crime was too low and
bestial—they perpetrated everything. And they had
so much influence they were greatly feared by the
Lisu. The power of life and death was supposed
to be only in the hands of the Chinese magistrate,
but as these magistrates were just as unprincipled,
a bribe would take care of any little overstepping
of authority. Comparatively speaking, the central
Chinese government knew little of what went on
in the canyon. Taxes were sent to the provincial
governor and the Salween was forgotten by the
world—but not by the Communists. The first rule

of Communist doctrine is to unsettle the territory they wish to commandeer, by brigandage, robbing raids, and so on. They deliberately use bandits, though they may repudiate them later.

We had been settled in Village of the Olives only four months when this first step of approaching Communism manifested itself in the uprising led by Dai Yi-gwan. He was attempting to flee to the nearest communist camp when Laird Dwan's men shot him.

By 1949 the Communists were already entrenched in the Mekong Valley (over the mountains east of Oak Flat), and in the Luda district to the north of us, and in the Salween Canyon itself. But Laird Dwan's reputation for deviltry and courage, coupled with his victory over Dai Yi-gwan, made them proceed toward our section of the canyon with caution.

This year of 1949 the church had changed the dates of the Rainy Season Bible School from the usual June, July, and August, to March, April, and May. Also it was held in the Village of the Olives for the first time. The Christians in this village had built a big church on Lucius' ground, and he had built a large five-room adobe house just above the church in which one hundred Lisu students were able to sleep. Thus schoolroom and dormitory were taken care of. Our bamboo shanty was next door to Lucius' new house.

We were in the midst of our three months of study when news came of the Dai Yi-gwan brigand group. We heard of the fall of Six Treasuries; the dividing of the group—one party led by Dai Yi-gwan went after Laird Dwan; the second party crossed the river to capture a smaller official at Luchang. The Chinese magistrate, who lived in

Luchang, fled into Burma at their approach, and it was he, returning with a regiment of soldiers, who finally drove out this group of brigands.

Luchang is on the same bank of the Salween as Olives and only a morning's walk away. Dai Yi-gwan, after he had robbed Laird Dwan, intended to cross over, join this group, and lead them on to get us. John was away in Paoshan. He had planned to be with us but a similar group of brigands attacked Paoshan simultaneously with those attacking us and John was in the besieged city for two months—he could not get out! So Charles Peterson and I went on with the school.

News of the brigands reaching Luchang and Laird Dwan's unexpected victory reached us on what we called our long weekend. When Communion Sunday occurred the students were always sent extra far away so as to administer it in villages which seldom had a special speaker. Thus this week end they were gone one day longer than usual. I remember that we wondered if those who had gone north would dare return to us, for it meant the brigands were only a morning's walk away from Olives and they had sent word they meant to come to us. Especially did I wonder about Teacher Philemon. It so happened on that particular week end that he had been assigned to his own home village of Lameh, far away and safely high up the mountain. Wouldn't they conclude that RSBS would have to disband, and stay home?

But Sunday night Philemon was one of the first back.

"Didn't you hear the news?" I asked him. "Don't you know the brigands are only half a day away?"

"Sure," he answered. "That's the very reason I

returned! To take care of you and Danny, Ma-ma. Are you going to flee? Will you come to my house?"

Bless him! It was comradeship like that which made life sweet, and knit us all together as one family.

Not one student stayed away! Popeyed with the excitement of what to do next, still they had all returned, so we continued our school. And then the Lord did the thing so unusual and so perfectly timed that we delight to call it a miracle. It was getting toward May, always the driest and hottest month of the year just before June when the rainy season starts. But it began to rain. Not gentle April showers but deluges day after day, day after day. In the back of our house Lucius' mother had planted a pumpkin crop, and the leaves were huge. Every morning when Danny and I awoke in the loft where we slept, we lay and listened to the *plop, plop* of heavy rain on those big leaves. This unprecedented downpour for some two weeks caused the streams, tributaries of the Salween, to swell and become raging torrents. There were several such between us and Luchang, and the brigands could not get across to us! Never could I remember such deluges day after day—it made me think of how Noah must have felt listening to such a downpour on the roof of the ark. It was miserable weather to do anything except teach the Bible! But we all grinned at one another and said, "This is God's protection."

Strange to say, before the rains became heavy, a letter from John was handed to me by a villager of Olives who had gone to Luchang to market. This letter had been *brought to Luchang by one of the brigands.* It seems he was brother to a little Christian girl in Paoshan and, hearing what her brother's gang was planning, she suggested John write me a letter and her brother bring it—otherwise we would not have known why John had not arrived! In the letter he explained they were besieged and he could not get out of the city, but was having a wonderful opportunity to witness to the frightened populace. That brother-letter-carrier was later executed in Pao-shan.

One memory of those sopping wet days was that of Abraham leading the student body in soldier drills for exercise. They had to get some exercise and outside was a hopeless mud slide. Now Abraham was a Nepalis who had been led to the Lord by Christian Lisu in Burma. He had been enlisted in Nepal by the Gurkha regiment, brought to Burma to fight the Japanese, and abandoned when the regiment broke up at the end of the war. Not all armies pay their soldiers' way back home when war is over!

We had a group of students from Burma that year, and Abraham was the grand solution to the problem of how to get exercise despite the rain. Lucius' big house had a long, covered porch, and there Captain Abraham marshaled his forces at the end of the day's school. While in the army he had learned that English child's game, "This is the way we march! This is the way we jump!"—followed by the action. Danny grabbed a stick for a gun and joined in enthusiastically, picking up Abraham's accent along with the game. I was dismayed to hear our little American son going around singing, "Dish is de vay ve march . . . dish is de vay ve jump!" and so on.

By the time the school concluded the brigands had been driven away, and a few weeks later John was back home. But to the north of us, right in the canyon, the Communists were in charge and threatening to descend upon us. It was only their fear of Laird Dwan which held them back. Nevertheless the work of the church went on. In the autumn it was necessary for John to make a trip to Kunming for reprints of our books, the *Catechism, First Steps in Reading,* and so on. At Christmas time many would want to buy these and we were all sold out. But by Christmas there were Communist uprisings all over the province and again John was cut off from us and could not get back. This time there was no brigand-messenger by whom to send a letter, so we had no notion why he did not arrive as promised. There is no telegraph in the canyon, of course.

The story of our bloody Christmas of 1949 has been told in detail in *Stones of Fire.* I will not repeat it here except to say that the Communists chose the Christian festival for their date of "liberation," as they so miscall it. Christmas is the one time of the year when farm work is slack and Christians from all over the canyon gather for three days of worship and celebration. This year it was to be held in Village of the Olives, and it was to Olives that the Communists came.

I was warned ahead of time by a note; besides this, Gaius, a deacon at Sandalwood Flat Village, met the band while on a trading trip. He told me they had a few armed Chinese soldiers but also they had a large number of *Lo-zi-lo-pa* with them. Now these *Lo-zi-lo-pa* were heathen Lisu robbers noted for their ruthless cruelty. The Communists, fearing Laird Dwan's cunning and machine guns (he had lately purchased some new ones to get ready for this fight), had brought the *Lo-zi-lo-pa* with them as a reserve, so to speak.

I had heard of these *Lo-zi-lo-pa* from the mother-in-law of Dateh John. Many years before she had been driving goats to market when she met a band of them. They not only stole her goats but they put her left hand on a rock and with another rock pounded it almost to a pulp. Then they tied her in the river up to her neck and left her. Wanton brutality. She showed me her hand, which dangled uselessly from her wrist for the rest of her life.

Those were the *Lo-zi-lo-pa* who were coming toward us! The note urged me not to flee, promising my safety. At the same time Laird Dwan was making his preparations. He waited until the Communists had really entered Olives; then, leading his men by cowpaths high up the mountain banks of the dell, he opened fire from ambush. Three or four were killed; the rest fled. By Christmas Eve, Olives was once more in the hand of our feudal laird, young Dwan. These were the two knives of the scissors—and we who lived in Olives were between them.

Christmas Day, Dwan and his soldiers withdrew, and then came word that the Reds planned to let loose the *Lo-zi-lo-pa* upon us, to kill and plunder as they liked in revenge for the fact that it was the headman of Olives who had apprised Laird Dwan of their arrival.

Now we were in real danger—horrible danger. Laird Dwan would not come to our rescue. He had just received word that the governor of Yunnan had turned the whole province over to the Communists! Now under Communist rule himself, he must make peace with them as best he might. He certainly would not try to defend us.

As I have said before, the mountain on which Village of the Olives stands is border country. This side is China, that side is Burma. But the road right over our mountain is such terrible climbing that no mule could go. So we usually go by way of Pien Ma Pass, as I could not walk such country for very long.

I knew by now that I must take Danny home to America. He was six years old, and was beginning to understand the vile heathen speech around him. At Oak Flat we had a large front and back garden fenced in—it was fairly simple to segregate him with a few children of Christians with whom he could safely play. At Olives we were right in the center of the village, with no fence, and no way to control which type became his playmates. One day in the kitchen Danny told me he wasn't going to Heaven. When I asked him why not, he answered darkly, "If you want me to be Jesus' boy, don't let me outside that door!" nodding to the one door of our shanty. Then I knew I must get him away. I taught him the Calvert Course every morning, but it was impossible to imprison such a lively youngster in such a small shanty.

Of course I had inquired about getting him to our own China Inland Mission School now moved to Kuling. But it was too late. Our secretary, Mr. Frank Parry, wrote me from Kunming. "The Generalissimo's planes bomb Kunming airport every day. To get to Kuling is now impossible."

So refugeeing through Burma and then to America seemed my only way. Knowing that probably I would be shut up to this route I had long before written to our home director asking that he contact the American Baptist Mission in Myitkyina, promising to refund any monies that I might need to draw from them in case I had to evacuate. I had an answer from Headquarters assuring me that the letter would be sent.

I had been saving silver currency to pay the carriers Danny and I would need for that long trek through the jungles of Upper Burma. I had money enough, and was ready to flee in every respect but two. The Lord had not told me to go. And I did not like to go without seeing John again.

But the *Lo-zi-lo-pa* were descending upon us! Surely that was guidance enough? It was insanity to stay. It was now that my bitter lesson of 1942 *in running too soon* stood me in good stead. The flesh loves excitement. It is always ready to jump up and run somewhere! It pushes and hurries us into action. The Holy Spirit does not. He is from the God of peace and His directions are always on time.

Someone has said, "Satan rushes men. God leads them." And Dr. F. B. Meyer has these potent words on this subject:

> Never act in panic, nor allow man to dictate to thee; calm thyself and be still; force thyself into the quiet of thy closet until the pulse beats normally and the scare has ceased to disturb. *When thou art most eager to act is the time when thou wilt make the most pitiable mistakes.* Do not say in thine heart what thou wilt or wilt not do, but wait upon God until He makes known His way. So long as that way is hidden, it is clear that there is no need of action, and that He accounts Himself responsible for all the results of keeping thee where thou art.

Another experienced saint once said: "The natural way is to rush at things. Hurry! Hurry! The supernatural way is to tarry! Tarry! Tarry! It is there the power from on high possesses us."

But how will the power from on high possess me? Wait on Him. The guidance will come different ways at different times. God is not confined to any one method, not even to using Scripture verses. I use a Scripture calendar ("Choice Gleanings" is my favorite) and the verse that morning was, *"Leave not thy place"* (Eccles. 10:3). Very appropriate. Just like an answer. But Satan could use an appropriate calendar verse too, or a Bible verse. Opening the Bible at random is not defended from his manipulations.

Whatever is given must be spoken in His voice. And you only learn to discern His voice by experience. If you want to be able to hear it in the crises of life you must first seek it in the common places of life. It is not suddenly acquired. *Selah*.

On this occasion, with the threat of the ruthless *Lo-zi-lo-pa* descending on us, I felt the verse was from Him. And after deciding not to flee I had perfect peace—another sign that it was His voice. If we have made a mistaken choice the Holy Spirit will most assuredly disturb us about it. If peace of heart follows, we can be sure it is of Him.

And so it proved. Day after day passed in quietness. What was happening we did not know. As a matter of fact, the laird's messenger, asking for a peace conference, arrived just in time to prevent the *Lo-zi-lo-pa* starting out to wreak revenge.

At length the Communist representatives to the peace conference arrived and by that we knew the threat of vengeance was lifted. Again the Lisu who had promised to escort Danny and me out through Burma urged me to go. The weather was perfect for traveling. With February would come rain on the lower slopes, snow on the heights, and the Pien Ma Pass might close for several months. Again I was tempted to go, but again I felt a restraint in the spirit—nothing tangible; something like the light touch of a hand holding me by the shoulder, so to speak. I just had no freedom in the spirit to leave.

And then one day (January 8, 1950) without warning, John arrived! And he had brought Eva, now graduated, with him! Oh, what a wonderful reunion!

There was so much to hear and tell. John had been held up by fighting on the Burma Road. But he had with him the coveted *Catechisms*—hundreds of them—and other printed matter. I told him of my contemplated trip to America to take Danny to school. He agreed, but thought that if I went soon, before the Communists had *organized* those distant parts, I might get back in again. But before Dan and I left he suggested a February Bible school, inviting students from Luda and all over. The Cookes had now evacuated to America (Mrs. Cooke had been ill) so there were no missionaries in the Luda district. To our great joy there was a hearty response and that last session of RSBS was the best one I ever knew. One hundred students gathered—two had to leave before the end. And when we sent them out during the week ends, to evangelize the villages to the north, the response was almost unbelievable. Hundreds of conversions were reported each week end. And the new *Catechisms* sold like hot cakes. The reason was an earthly one—the Communists had said that the Christians were the only honest citizens in the canyon! But at least it gave us a chance to teach the Truth to these who had never given it an unprejudiced hearing before.

Little Nurse Eva went right to work on the medical side. With almost no equipment and only a very smoky charcoal fire to sterilize instruments, she did operations on sick eyes by herself, and was so successful that her fame spread far and wide. As usual she would make only a nominal charge to the Lisu for her skill—fifty cents or a dollar, I think it was.

When they brought her a capon or eggs in their deep gratitude she turned it over to us, insisting that the family eat them with her.

At the end of the school, Danny and I had to make preparations for our departure. It would be two weeks' trekking through the jungles of Upper Burma. John offered to go with us, but with all these new converts to supervise I felt he should not come. When Lucius offered to be my escort, we decided to accept him.

The parting with Daddy was one of the hardest we had ever had. I felt myself that I would not get back, that Communism would never allow evangelistic Christianity to work under their regime. John is an optimist by nature, but when it came to saying good-by, for once he could not force a smile. We left him on a high rock jutting out from the road, biting his lips in grim determination. And we set our faces toward a trek that must take us halfway around the world. But that is for the next chapter.

The knives of the scissors are like two dangers or two painful situations which, to human sight, must cut us in pieces when they finally met. What is our refuge there? It must be to shut our eyes tight to the physical situation as the mere outward eye sees it. Our refuge must be to get absolutely quiet in the inner man so that God can speak, then direction will be given. The experience may be compared to tightrope walking. The walker must be trained on easy, low ropes first. When he is trained to throw off all the glamorous outside calls and attend to that one thing, his eye on that one goal, then only he is ready to put his training to the test in the place of danger. We must learn first, to-day, now, in this smaller easier matter, to walk with our eyes on the Lord only. Only then can we do it victoriously under the later high tension of danger or excitement.

First I had to learn to *fear* running away before God's time had come. Then I had to learn to discern His voice from the hurry-hurry voices of the flesh, and to hold on in steadfast patience.

If I had run off to Burma when *the Lo-zi-lo-pa* scare came, see what I would have lost:

1. I would have missed seeing John.

2. I would have missed meeting Eva. (I never saw her again. She had to stay behind in China, when at length John was ordered out of the canyon.)

3. I would have missed the repentance of Keh-deh-seh-pa.

4. I would have missed that last wonderful RSBS session where hundreds of heathen Lisu were garnered in.

These platforms, or struggles in life, do not necessarily make us stronger Christians. I want to be sure this is understood. Many victories do not make a stronger Christian. It does give us an experience of Christ's ability to help us, so the next time it is easier to trust Him. But it is fatal to think that we have become strong. Oswald Chambers used to say he feared to become forty, for so many once shining Christians seem to grow cold or flabby in their spiritual lives at that age. Maybe it was because they thought themselves strong and unconsciously released the flesh from the position of crucifixion.

Platforms do not make us stronger Christians or better Christians but they do make us *richer* Christians. Rich in our inner fellowship with Him. Rich in our confidence that He will be our Rock and our Deliverer in the future. Rich in the relaxation of the little child who leans back on his father's breast, confident, secure, and satisfied.

> Oh, the deep, deep love of Jesus,
>   Love of every love the best:
> 'Tis an ocean vast of blessing
>   'Tis a haven sweet of rest.
> Oh, the deep, deep love of Jesus
>   'Tis a heaven of heaven to me;
> And it lifts me up to glory
>   For it lifts me up to Thee.
>   —S. T. FRANCIS

CHAPTER ELEVEN

STRANDED AT WORLD'S END

A<small>ND NOW</small> D<small>ANNY AND</small> I were on our way to America. First came the Pien Ma Pass (10,998-foot elevation). We left Village of the Olives on March 10. That night we slept in rice fields by the side of the Salween River. March 11 we climbed, pressed through the town of Luchang, and learned that the new Communist official was due to arrive the next week. He would never have allowed us to leave, of course, so we escaped just in time. The third day we were still climbing but now on the sides of the great Pien Ma Mountain itself. That night we slept in a hamlet called Er-tso-cho, the last house on the slopes below the Pass. And the next morning when I woke up early, to my dismay I heard the pitter-patter of rain on the roof! That meant it was snowing on the Pass, and the trail across the top would be obliterated. All that day it rained, all the next night and all the next day! My carriers, dear Christian boys, most of them farmers in Olives, began to talk about going back home. Snow will have closed the Pass, they argued. And the weather looked like a ten-day rain, after which the ground would be just right for the first plowing. There was no use trying to get over the Pass, we must all turn around and go back to Olives!

You can imagine how I felt—and how I prayed.

To go back to Olives meant that Danny would have to go through the Communist ordeal after all—imprisonment or internment, not to speak of the moral dangers from Village of the Olives, two-thirds of which was still heathen. As a matter of fact, John was allowed wonderful freedom for one year after the Communist officials arrived. Then he was "invited" out at the point of a bayonet, and forced to trek all across China, although exit through Burma would have been so easy. In desperation I prayed, "Lord, if this obstacle is from Thee, I accept it; if it is from Satan I refuse it." As I prayed this, an idea came to me.

"Boys," I said, "if we turn back tomorrow to Olives because of the weather, *and then* the sun came out, wouldn't you feel foolish? And you know what a loss of money it would be to me. Now let us arrange this way and pray for God's guidance. If when we wake up tomorrow morning it is not raining we will take it as a sign to start out. On the other hand, when we reach the snow line, if it begins to snow or the trail is difficult to find, I will consent to turn back with you. I know that people perish every year trying to cross Pien Ma Pass in times of snow, and I have no wish to endanger you or ourselves. But I have found that if we go as far as we can, God often opens up the rest of the way. Will you do it?"

They agreed, for they were all Christians and we really had wonderful fellowship together. You can imagine how I strained my ears about cock-crow that next morning! There was silence. The pitter-patter on the roof had ceased. Throwing something over me I went to the door and looked out—not promising; heavy storm clouds lay low over the hills and the air was damp, *but it was not raining*. When I went back in, I found Lucius making the fire for breakfast, so I told him to call the others to get up, that we would start out. No one looked thrilled.

"The trail will be obliterated, Ma-ma, after two days and nights of such a snowstorm," Lucius warned quietly.

"If it is, I will turn back with you," I promised, "but let us go and see." I counted much on the fact that it was not actually raining—the sign I had asked from God. So we set out. Our host at this last cabin, the last human outpost before the final climb, was loud in protestations that we would never make it—which did not help the boys to feel any happier.

As we began that climb which would take us all the morning, the sun shot forth in one golden stream upon us. But it was only for a moment, then it disappeared behind clouds and a thin drizzle of rain descended! We were climbing through dark and lonely vegetation, up and up. The rain stopped but we were among the clouds by now, which as you know, is like being in a fog. It is wet and depressing. I was riding our mule, Jasper, and Danny was being carried in a mountain chair (like a stretcher but with a seat instead of a bed) on the shoulders of Canaan and Daniel. The Lisu, usually so merry and cheerful on the road, were silent, and I was wondering if it was right for me to endanger their lives; should I call a halt and turn back? I was praying for guidance when through the fog, up above us on the rocky ascent, loomed two black figures. They spied us as we spied them and both parties shouted. The next instant they were down beside us—two Lisu heathen of the Luda district. They were returning from a trading trip in Burma and had just crossed over the Pass!

"How's the top?" our men shouted.

"The snow is deep, but we are a large party. You can find your way by our footprints if you hurry. *Ah beh!* Didn't we first fellows have a time!" Delighted that their lives were spared, for the trail would be easy from now on, they sprang on down the slope, passing us.

"When you reach Village of the Olives, tell Mapa you saw us!" I called to them.

"We'll do that," they called back, then the cloud swallowed them up.

Now our men pushed upward with new vigor. Farther on two more of this Luda party met us.

"It's beginning to snow on the top of the Pass," one of them answered our eager inquiries, "but you can make it. Watch for our footprints; there is nothing else to show where the trail is."

It was now noon and all of us were hungry but we did not dare to waste time making a fire and cooking lunch. I had one slice of bread left and a small piece of cheese. This I divided with Danny when we finally arrived at the top of Pien Ma Pass. It usually presents a most marvelous view, with China spread out before you on the one side and Burma on the other! But now almost all was covered with snow clouds. On the China side the sun was trying to struggle through, but on the Burma side all was dark and lowering. In fact, it was beginning to snow in tiny half-wet flakes which melted immediately they touched us.

The trail over the top of Pien Ma Pass is but a cowpath in width. It winds back and forth on the level for a short distance before plunging down into the steep descent. We met more Luda Lisu shivering as they struggled on toward the China side, but their feet had sunk deeply into the snow, marking out the trail for us. It was God's provision. We waited until our party was all together, the slower ones catching up with us who led the way, then we began to cross the Pass. We had not gone far when Jasper suddenly sank to his stomach in snow. I had to dismount. With Samson pulling at his head, and Lucius jerking him by the tail, they finally got the mule out and onto the trail again where the snow was not so deep. I climbed on his back once more but heard a call from behind me.

"May we carry Danny pickaback, Ma-ma? We can't make it with this big awkward chair."

"All right," I called back as Jasper floundered and snorted and the snowstorm grew thicker and heavier.

So one of the Lisu carried Danny on his back and Daniel carried the empty chair. Danny had a raincoat and rubber hat on so the snow-sleet dripped off him easily. He was the most comfortable one of the whole party and cheered the rest of us by singing at the top of his voice!

As for me, the snow melted off me and ran into my galoshes. Soon my feet were in pools of snowwater and I lost all feeling up to the knees. I was soaked to the waist too, for my plastic raincoat kept slipping back off my knees.

Of course as we reached lower altitudes the snow changed to rain, the steep path became muddy and slippery. Finally Jasper could not keep his feet, but began to slide dangerously.

"You will have to get off, Ma-ma," said Samson at last. So I had to jump off, trusting that my feet would hold me up, although I had lost all feeling in them. Lucius helped me and so we continued to slip and slide in descent. It was half-past four in the afternoon before we reached the pretty valley where Pien Ma Village nestled. Pink peach blossoms were beginning to burst into lovely color against the new green of spring buds, and everything was shining from the recent rain-wash.

But nobody invited us into their homes! "There are a couple of guest houses up the hill there," we were told coolly and pointed to two empty shacks which did not look in very good repair. There was nothing to do but camp in them as best we could. We asked to buy some firewood but what they gave us was green and smoked badly. Our bedding was quite wet in spots and with the smoky fire we could not get it dry. But we were out of Communist China! True, we had no visa to enter Burma; we still had ten days' trek through the jungle before we came upon civilization; and even after we reached Myit-kyina Danny and I would still be halfway across the world from home. There was plenty to think about. But at least we were over the Pass.

Supper over, a bed for the night was the next problem. There were no beds in the huts so we all slept on the bamboo floor around the central fire-place. Our bedding was still streaked with damp. I chose the dry spots for Danny and wrapped him up well but I had to lie down on part of the quilt and cover with none-too-dry blankets. Then the storm began again with violence. It hailed outside once and then rain came spatting down. Every now and again it spat through the leaks of the roof onto our faces, and altogether it was a depressing situation. I knew it was snowing hard on the Pass and as it blew hard all night, by morning the Pass would be closed. In other words, we were shut up to going forward. But what if I got lumbago from sleeping in damp bedding? I had caught it some years before and that time the bedding was drier than this. With lumbago I could not walk or ride a horse all day no matter how I summoned my will power. I was helplessly cast upon the Lord.

Was I really in His will to come? This time He had given me no Bible verse on which to lean. I had asked for one but none came. It would have been so comfortable to have a Bible verse to stand upon as in my experience of 1942. This was eight years later, and God expects His children to *grow*. I believe it was D. E. Hoste who said that the older he grew the harder it seemed to get guidance from the Lord. I believe he meant that guidance becomes less simple. God expects us to exercise spiritual discernment, and He guides by a certain pressure on the spirit, by a still small voice, by a something so delicately intangible that unless you are carefully tuned in to His Spirit, so to speak, you can miss it widely. It requires a close and experienced walk with the Lord, so in one sense, He has a hold on us that might not be if He always supplied us with a Bible verse every time we asked for one!

When it is only a still small voice which is our guide, it is easy for Satan to throw us into confusion by causing us to question if we heard aright. It is a good plan not to go back on past guidance. Yet how patient is our Master! He does not desert us even then. I did *not* get lumbago or even rheumatism, and we had to travel in the rain more than once after that, for the storm continued. As we journeyed through the mountains Danny asked

me to sing "The Ninety and Nine," for I happened
to remember all the verses. And when we came to

Then all through the mountains thunder-riven,
And up from the rocky steep—

he would join in with great gusto. *"The mountains,*
thunder-riven," seemed our daily diet!

But the road was not as bad as maybe you are
thinking. True, it took us through the jungles of
Upper Burma, but the British (when in power in
Burma) had caused fairly good roads to be cut
and maintained through to Pien Ma Pass, and every
ten or fifteen miles they had built rest houses. These
were simple rustic bungalows built in a clearing
in the jungle and had a native caretaker in charge.
There were beds (without mattresses or bedding;
every traveler carried his own), and a table and
chair, and the caretaker could cook a decent meal.
The Japanese had destroyed the rest houses nearer
to the border, so we did not come across any for
several days. Once we did so, however, I began to
feel in clover, sure of a clean good rest at night.
But before we reached these, we arrived at a place
where lived a Lisu Christian from the Salween. We
stayed at his house and the next morning a message
reached us. Mrs. Kuhn was to report to the Burmese
official immediately. Knowing I had no visa to enter
Burma I had to comply, although it meant saddling
Jasper and riding back up the mountain to the official's residence. The effort proved to be well worth
it, however.

The official was a Karen and a Christian. He told
me so himself almost as soon as he had greeted me.
He gave me some good advice about what to do, in
my visa-less state. I must report to the police as

soon as I arrived at any point of importance—Myitkyina or Rangoon. By short-wave radio he must advise the police at Myitkyina of my approach. But he
also sent word to the American Baptist missionary
in residence at Myitkyina, Rev. Herman Tegenfeldt,
who perhaps would be able to meet us with his
jeep; there was a motor road that would save us two
days' travel if we could get a vehicle on it. I thanked
the official, and our party went back down the hill
and on our way.

That night as I registered at the rest house I
was startled and thrilled to see in a very familiar
handwriting: *Mr. and Mrs. Orville Carlson.* I knew
the Carlsons were hoping to go to Goomoo and teach
the Maru-Kachin whom Mark had led to the Lord
(a thousand of them had believed before Mark
died), but I had not heard for sure that they got
out of Yunnan before it fell to the Communists. We
had missed them by only one week, but it was a
jolt of joy to know there was somebody in Burma
whom I knew!

In between those rest houses the road was often
cut through heavy jungle. Wild animals abounded.
The fresh spoor of a tiger lay on the dew-soft earth
one early morning as we started out. We all had
to keep together at such times, but the Lord protected us all the way.

At last we reached the motor road and the rest
house beside it. Some of our Lisu had never seen
a truck, and I was hoping I could pay a driver to
give them a little ride. A government rice truck
drove in the very evening we arrived, and the driver
had a short trip to make the next morning. He would
take the Lisu with him and from there they could
go on to Myitkyina on foot. They could leave their

loads behind, for he would return and get us and the baggage and drive us to Myitkyina. On the strength of that promise Samson and the mountain-chair carriers asked permission to be allowed to set out on their return journey back into China. The mule could not go on the truck, someone must go back with it, and these Lisu were not interested in seeing Myitkyina anyway.

So the next morning we said good-by to them, and cheered off the excited group who were to have their first auto ride! Lucius was the only one left with Danny and me. Imagine our chagrin when about noon we received a telephone message at the rest house saying that the truck had broken down, but as the driver had assured the Lisu other trucks would take us, the dear Lisu were not returning to us! This did leave us in a predicament—all our heavy baggage with us and no carriers! We inquired about a truck and were told they did not come fre-quently—perhaps one a week.

All the following morning we waited and prayed, so you can imagine our feelings when about noon we heard a motor toot down the road. We all ran out to look, and there was a red jeep with a white man at the wheel coming merrily toward us. Mr. Tegenfeldt and two of his children, Alice and John! They had brought a picnic lunch, beautifully pre-pared by his dear wife. And at the sight of those fine sandwiches wrapped in wax paper, I felt that I had reached civilization at last!

Myitkyina is perhaps the most important city in Upper Burma. It has an airport and the Irrawady River flows by it. Here the Tegenfeldts live and from here, with its city church and school, they also keep in touch with a large country work among the tribes. There are several other tribes which are ranked higher than the Lisu in intelligence and tribal culture. Mr. Tegenfeldt supervised work in all of these.

But one of my first questions was concerning that letter which Headquarters had promised to write to Mr. Tegenfeldt, guaranteeing a refund of any sums of money advanced to me. No such letter had come, said Mr. Tegenfeldt. I cannot tell you the dismay and alarm that filled me.

The title of this chapter may sound far-fetched to the reader but it is descriptive of my *feelings* rather than my actual condition. I was now at the other end of the world from home. I had practically no Burmese money, did not speak their language, and had no one in the whole country to guarantee me. I was in a turmoil of questions and I felt stranded at the end of the world.

Well, the first thing is to *cast out fear*. The only fear a Christian should entertain is the fear of sin. All other fears are from Satan, sent to confuse and weaken us. How often the Lord reiterated to His disciples, "Be not afraid!" So, alone in our bedroom in the Tegenfeldts' nice home, I knelt by the bed and spread my heart before Him. I refused to be afraid and asked Him to cast such fears out of my heart.

Then I must seek light for the next step. I must report to the Burmese police, but after that I would need to find a way to get some money. We still had some of Grandpa Kuhn's legacy in the bank of John's home town, Manheim, Pennsylvania. I had blank checks with me, but who would believe that I really had the money there? Would the Tegenfeldts trust me? They had never met me before and only knew that there was a Kuhn family working in the Salween Canyon.

Rather timidly I asked Mr. Tegenfeldt if he could cash a check for me—quite a large check, because I found that Danny and I would have to fly to Rangoon. The railroad had been bombed and there were no through trains.

"No, I don't think I can," replied Mr. Tegenfeldt. "Why don't you go on the street and try to sell it?" He did not even offer to come along and guarantee me, but I found out later why he seemed so unconcerned—he knew an endorser would not be required and probably did not guess my doubts!

So, with Lucius for company, and the little book of blank checks on a small-town bank in America, I started down the business street looking for some shop where someone might speak English! We had not gone far when a tall Hindu, bearded and turbaned, smiled and said, "Good morning!" Timidly I entered his shop and produced my book. "I am a missionary," I said. "Would you cash a check for me?"

"For how much?" he inquired gravely.

"For $150.00 American?" I replied.

He took the check and looked at it a moment. "Is this negotiable in India?"

"Yes," I replied. "It can be cashed anywhere."

"All right," he answered, and in five minutes a roll of Burmese money was in my hand! Just as easy as that. No one had even asked to see my passport. I felt like Alice in Wonderland, as I returned jubilant to the Tegenfeldt's home. Apparently Christian missionaries are so trusted in Burma that they can cash a check anywhere without a guarantor!

I know of no other country in the world where this can be done.

Well, so far so good. Now to get to Rangoon. Mr. Tegenfeldt took me to the police and helped me with all the red tape involved. In fact, no one could have been kinder than Ruth and Herman Tegenfeldt were to us in every way.

Word had gone around that Ma-ma and Danny were in Myitkyina and a large group of Lisu came to see us, including Abraham (the Nepalis), men who had been in our RSBS, and others who had fled to Burma when the brigand scare was on. We had a precious time together.

But at Rangon—where would Danny and I stay? The Tegenfeldts gave us the address of a missionary guest house where they always stayed, and I wired to inquire if they could accommodate Danny and me. But I received no answer. Lucius and another Lisu boy rode with us to the airport and it was hard to say good-by. I felt I might never see him again on earth, and I have not.

But just before we boarded the plane, a note was handed to me by passengers getting off it. Once we were up in the air I opened it and saw it was signed, *Eric Cox*. Oh, how I thanked the Lord! Eric had been working among the Atsi-Kachin tribe far south of us in Yunnan. (His dear wife, Grace Liddell Cox, had died on furlough.) I knew that he too hoped to go home to America to see his children, and that he planned to go via Burma, but I did not know when he was leaving. The note said that he was at the guest house when my telegram arrived and, hearing the hostess say she had no room for us, he had made arrangements for us to stay with the Bible Churchmen's Missionary So-

ciety's Deaf School and he hoped to meet us at the
airport!

What could have been more wonderful! Psalm
59:10 (A.S.V.): *"My God with his lovingkindness
shall come to meet me,"* had been fulfilled again.
I was thrilled. Maybe we could travel on the same
ship with "Uncle" Eric, and Danny would have the
pleasure of his companionship. Eric had been a sea
officer when God called him to missionary service,
so there was nothing about a ship he would not be
able to teach a small boy.

But I still had an unknown adventure to go
through before we reached Rangoon.

The airplane was a freight plane, dirty and uncomfortable. We had been told we would come
down only once before Rangoon, that being at
Mandalay. But, lo, and behold, we came down at
Bhamo. Danny had gotten his hand into some black
grease so I took him off the plane hoping to find
a washroom. Bhamo was a flat, hot place with some
Burmese officials standing in a group talking. Low
one-storied buildings were in the background.

Just then a jeep drove up. In it were two white
people, dust-covered and looking like—well, like *missionaries.* Glad to meet my own kind I was approaching them when they sprang and almost ran to me.

"You're a misisonary? Your name, please?" asked
the lady.

"Mrs. John Kuhn, from China."

"Oh, we know your husband! He visited us at
Namkham last year. I am Grace Seagrave and this
is my brother, Gordon."

Of course I had heard of the famous Seagrave
family. I bowed and, indicating Danny's dirty hand,
was about to ask where the washroom was when

Dr. Grace said, "Oh, Gordon will take him and wash him up." Which Dr. Gordon did.

All this time Dr. Grace was chattering anything and everything and coming so close to me that I instinctively backed up. I did not see at first that she was deliberately doing this to back me up to a place where we would be alone and not overheard by the curious Burmese official group. When she had me backed away from them and up against the side of the plane she suddenly produced a letter and said, "We have had trouble at Namkham Hospital. There has been a Karen uprising and Gordon is falsely charged with helping them. Our mail is all intercepted and we cannot get our side of the affair out to our friends. We drove sixty miles today in the hope there would be someone on this plane who would take this letter for us to the American Consul in Rangoon. It explains our side. Quick! Have you got a pocket in your skirt or somewhere to put it?

Political intrigue? This was the last thing I wanted to get mixed up in—I with no visa for Burma and having to report to the police as soon as I arrived in Rangoon! I faltered in reply, praying inwardly, "O Lord, direct me what to do!" Now, unknown to Dr. Grace, there was a Burmese official walking up and down behind her, watching our every move. Just as I prayed that, this official reached the end of his walk and had to turn to come back. Instead of turning toward us he turned *away* from us. In just that one second, I quickly opened the long pocketbook I held in my hand, Dr. Grace popped the letter into it, and when that man resumed his guard over us, there was nothing for him to see. Dr. Gordon Seagrave returned with

Danny, the call came to board the plane and—we were off. But now I carried on my person that which if discovered might have put me in prison. As you may know, Dr. Gordon Seagrave was put in prison later over this very affair. (I understand Dr. Grace Seagrave died the next year.)

There were some on the plane with us who spoke English and from them I learned that there was usually a minute baggage examination at Rangoon. But we were late getting in. When finally we arrived, only one immigration-customs officer remained and he was anxious to get home.

"Only your personal things, I expect?" he said, indicating our baggage.

"Yes, sir."

"O.K. I won't ask you to open them. Passed!" and he left us. So the Lord delivered me. At a later time in Rangoon they asked to see into my pocketbook too, but by then the Seagrave letter was safely in the hands of the American Consul. I delivered it into his own hand myself, and the next year when the affair came out in *Time* magazine, I had the satisfaction of knowing that at least the Seagrave side of the matter had been presented to American authorities.

And now for the BCMS Deaf School where we were so kindly received by Miss Sturman and her fellow worker. Eric Cox had missed us at the airport but came around the next morning and took me to downtown Rangoon, to the police station, to the immigration offices, to the American Consulate— everywhere. He had just been through the red tape for himself so knew where the various buildings were located and how to help me.

I had hoped we could get passage from Ran-

goon, but learned that ships were so few I would
need to book space six months ahead. The only
other way out was to fly to Hong Kong and try
for a freighter there. Eric himself was doing this
and soon had to leave us, but he promised to telegraph if there was possibility of our getting on the
same ship.

The China Inland Mission had a treasurer stationed at Hong Kong, so that once there our money
problems ended; we would be able to draw on
him for what we needed.

The telegram came: BOAT LEAVING SATURDAY. ERIC.
We read it with a sigh for we could not possibly
make it by then. Being a Canadian, I was having
to go through a long process to get into the United
States, including a physical examination and shots
for this and for that, which had to have intervals of
time in between them and could not be hurried.
So we had to relinquish hope of having "Uncle"
Eric on the same ship with Danny.

At length we were through and ready to fly to
Hong Kong. The only bookings we could get were
on the Siamese Airways, and these had a stopover
of one day in Bangkok.

Siam, or Thailand as it is now called, did not interest me much. It never entered my head that I
would ever return there! To me it was merely a
36-hour stopover. Danny and I, for some unknown
reason, were not booked at the same hotel as the
other passengers, but were sent to the Ratanakosin—
the most modern and expensive hotel in Bangkok.
We arrived on the Saturday when Eric Cox was to
sail out of Hong Kong. The next day was April 9—
Easter Sunday!

Danny was very thrilled with the elevator in the

hotel. He remembered them from Dallas days but got the English name mixed up with *alligator* and caused many a smile in the big lobby by calling out, "Mamma, I want to go up in the alligator!"

I inquired about English church services but could get no information from the desk clerk, so we ventured forth to try and find the missionary community. Bangkok uses pedicabs, which are like rickshas except that the driver pedals a tricycle instead of walking. We finally found the American Bible Society, where Mr. and Mrs. Marvin Martin received us cordially and invited us to dinner. There was no English service until night, and as I wished to get Danny to bed in preparation for an early flight on Monday morning, I took him back to the Ratanakosin.

As we walked through the lobby the desk clerk called to me, "Telephone, Ma'am!" I wondered who could be calling me. It was the Siamese Airways.

"We find you do not have a visa for Hong Kong for your son, Daniel, Mrs. Kuhn. You may not proceed tomorrow."

"But he is only six years old! He doesn't need a visa!" I gasped.

"When you get a visa for him you may proceed, and not until then, Madame," was the short reply, and they hung up.

My face must have betrayed my feelings, for Danny pulled at my skirt asking anxiously, "What is it, Mamma? What is it?"

"You don't have a visa for Hong Kong," was all I could answer, for my heart was like lead. I wanted to get out of sight and cry. Stranded in Bangkok and at the most expensive hotel! I pulled out my little checkbook on the home-town bank. "May I pay my bills by check?" I asked the clerk. You should have seen the contemptuous amusement on his face!

"No, Madame. You may pay in American cash or Siamese money. We do not accept checks."

I turned and sought the elevator and our bedroom. Once there I fell on my knees by the bed and sought the dear Lord. "O God, undertake for me!" I cried. "Whatever shall I do? I do not know a soul in this country. The Martins were kind to give us a meal but they are utter strangers. O Lord, speak to me!" and I pulled out my Bible and desperately opened it. There before me was Isaiah 65:24, "Before they call, I will answer."

"That is a very nice verse, dear Lord," I said, still uncomforted, "but how does it apply to us *now?*"

As I waited before Him, my memory was illumined. Why, of course! How could I have forgotten? Quickly I pulled my purse over to me and slipped back the zipper to an inner pocket. Yes, it was still there! An American ten- and a five-dollar bill. "Before they call." Our mail in China was so interrupted that we received only a few batches of it those last six months of 1949. But in two of those batches had been a card once and a note from a lady in California who was a stranger to me. With the note she had enclosed a five-dollar bill and with the Christmas card a ten-dollar bill. Both had come through safely, although brigands and robbers abounded. I could not use them in Lisuland, so I had put them into this secret pocket of my purse for use on the trip home but had forgotten them. That lady, the giver, I never did meet, and she has ceased to be interested in us since. But the Lord surely used her to our blessing that year.

From the depths of despair I was lifted into joyous worship of Him. How wonderful to find Him *always there*, when we have unexpected need of Him! That living touch with Him is so precious; it makes Him so real; it obliterates the line between the earthly and heavenly; it is so humbling to find Him *waiting there*. Our hotel bill, by the way, was just $10.00 U.S.!

On Easter Monday the British Consulate was open for only one hour in the morning, but time enough to obtain a visa. A visit to the Siamese Airways, and our passages for Tuesday were secured. The rest of the day was ours, and to my astonishment I found that it was a big day in Bangkok. It was the day appointed for King Phumiphon to cremate his uncle, and the ceremony was to take place in front of the Ratanakosin Hotel! From the roof garden we had a "box seat" view of it all.

A high conical platform, to which marble steps with brass railings led, was erected in the open park across from the hotel. The railings were hung with lacy green ferns and the top of the platform was roofed with gold and crimson. On the platform was the pyre. The procession was two hours long and a fascinating pageant in Oriental colors and splendor. The body arrived in an urn which was set in a carriage hung with gold curtains. Set to weird Buddhist music, the chantings of the priests filled the air and stirred the blood to excitement. All Thailand was represented in the companies which formed the long procession—the nobles, the priests, the police, the armed forces with all their divisions, and so on. Most fascinating were the cavalry whose beautiful horses were trained to do the dead march. The king was carried to the scene in a golden palanquin. And when all was set, he, dressed in a white uniform, mounted the marble stairs between the fern-hung brass railings—up, up, and up to the pyre at the top, where he kindled the fire. It was earth's glory at its most dramatic, but it contained no hope for the poor soul of the dead man, who before God's judgment seat must stand naked in his sins. There is no hush or reverence in a Buddhist funeral. There is only gaudy display and loud clamor to drown out thought.

Tuesday morning we boarded the plane for Hong Kong. A group of Chinese gentlemen got on with us, and we found we were to come down in Hainan. When we reached the island the co-pilot came back into the plane and spoke to us.

"As you see, we are circling over Hainan," he said. "We have important personnel on board and may not come down until the reception committee has reached the airfield." We circled for almost half an hour! Then down we came and the Chinese passengers got out. The reception committee was there and regiments of Nationalist soldiers were drawn up all over the field. Ten days later the Communists had taken the whole island.

Hong Kong at last! As Danny and I descended the gangplank we heard a shout, "Praise the Lord!" Looking to our right, over there behind wire netting was—Eric Cox, smiling and waving to us! And beside him Sally Harverson of old Yunnan days. But we had to go through immigration and customs first.

The immigration officer examined Danny's passport. "Oh, you are the people who were held up in Bangkok for the little boy's visa?"

"Yes, sir."

"Well, it wasn't needed. Juniors do not need a

visa to enter Hong Kong."

Why was it allowed? Satan trying to harass? I do not know. There are many apparently needless trials in life, but the Lord stands with us through all of them. "May you lose nothing in the furnace but your dross," said Samuel Rutherford. The Lord will preserve everything else for us.

He had even kept "Uncle" Eric for Danny's boat trip home! The boilers of the *Skauvann* had broken down and she was delayed just long enough to get Danny and me aboard. The lovingkindness of our Lord—"*Surely goodness and mercy shall follow me all the days of my life.*"

We had a great reception by wonderful friends in Vancouver, and the same from others as we passed through Seattle; then on by train to meet Kathryn at Wheaton (Ill.) College.

It was wonderful to see Kathryn again—now *grown up,* with an adult mind, and the ability to share life's problems with understanding. Our fellowship rose to a new level.

We arrived just a month before commencement—who could find a place to stay at Wheaton *then?* A student, sensing he would fail in his exams, suddenly went home and left a bedrom vacant in the very house where Mrs. Ella Graham had an apartment! So we had a room right near the college, and we ate with kind "Aunt" Ella.

A beautiful little college town in the heart of America! Long streets tree-shaded, with squirrels scampering happily from branch to branch. No air-raid alarms. No windows iron-barred against thieves. Just peace and plenty; the beauty of spring and gay young voices. Family life, friendships, freedom. It was like Heaven on earth; never will I forget it!

Halfway across the world He had brought us. Through snowy heights and wild jungle, bombed bridges and railroads; past suspicious immigration officials with endless red-tape regulations; soldiers, and tension everywhere. Chinese money, Burmese money, Siamese money, Hong Kong money—oh, let's never mention the word again! He had supplied as each need arose, but each time in a different way.

Stranded at world's end? Maybe. But if we lean back we will find ourselves on the bosom of Christ— sweet, familiar place.

> Sometimes on the Rock I tremble,
>   Faint of heart and weak of knee;
> But the steadfast Rock of Ages
>   Never trembles under me!

It was an enriching experience to have found Him living and quick to bless in those strange countries— Burma, Thailand, and Hong Kong. As Hudson Taylor commented when a newspaper reporter described him as leading a hand-to-mouth existence), "Yes, but it is from God's hand to my mouth." I ended up with being so glad that it happened just that way, that I might know again the thrill of *God's hand to my mouth.*

So the platform ended, with His power having been manifested to me again, and a fresh knowledge of Himself given.

> Darkness! But look! There's a Form in the night!
>   This fresh terror but grips them anew.
> Jesus calls out, "It is I, do not fear!"
>   Then what joy fills the heart of the crew!
> Over the turbulent waters He came,
>   The wind heard His unuttered command;
> Time was no more, as they worshiped the Lord,
>   For at once, they were safe on the land.
>   —M. J. C.

CHAPTER TWELVE

DREAD DISEASE

IF THE LORD TARRY, there must come, sometime, a last platform. Always the flesh would pray that it might be an easy one. But the Lord looks to the eternal weight of glory and so He may choose otherwise sometimes.

The story of how we were led to go to Thailand, after John was released by the Communists, has been told in *Ascent to the Tribes*.[1] The beginning of this chapter finds us there.

I think the very beginning is to be found in my first trip in search of the tribes of North Thailand. As we were climbing those hills on that occasion, hindrances, annoyances, accidents kept happening to our group until we decided they must come from the satanic forces which had ruled the heights above us since first human beings found their way there. We gathered together right there on the steep jungle-tangled mountainside and claimed the power of the blood over each member of our party.

It was not before, but after that prayer of faith, that I was suddenly struck in the breast by a stick. We were walking single file, and a fallen tree branch lay concealed under the leaves of the path. As the young worker in front of me unknowingly stepped

[1]By the same author. Moody Press, 1956.

on the one end, the other end sprang up and struck me severely.

When I could recover my breath and walk on (I was last in the line), I talked to the Lord in my heart.

"Lord, why did You let that happen? You know a blow like that to a woman fifty years of age is likely to turn to cancer. Was I not covered with Your precious blood?"

These thoughts came immediately.

"You *were* covered, dear. And it *will* turn to cancer. And I am going to use that to take you back to America."

Now it was not *clearly* His voice. I repeat, the Lord sometimes speaks so clearly that we *cannot confound or doubt Him, or deny.* This was not that. I did not dare say that those thoughts had been from Him. The parting with the children again had been hard, so the above thoughts might have been just the wishful thinking of the mother-part of me. Therefore I did not count on it being His voice. As soon as we returned to civilization, I went to Dr. Buker for examination. He felt it was just a torn ligament, so I accepted that diagnosis and went on with my work, deliberately putting all thoughts of serious trouble out of my mind.

Seven months passed, and again I was in the mountains, in quite a different part of the country and with a different group of fellow workers. We were preaching in a hamlet where I had never been before, and the headman's shanty was packed with Lisu villagers. John presented the Gospel to them, to which they listened attentively. Then he turned to me and said, "Now you preach for awhile." I felt I should tell them that Christ Jesus is stronger than the demons to whom they are so enslaved. Immediately it was as if a voice said, "Better not. If you do, the demons will take revenge on *you*." But I did proclaim that anyway, for it is a truth they much needed to know: *"If the Son shall make you free ye shall be free indeed."* I had no sooner said it, however, than the young men all jumped up in alarm and left the house—leaving me speaking to only women and children!

When I had finished, our party departed from the village, but as we did so someone said, "Look up at that demon shrine!" On the hill above us were young men silently encircling their shrine as if on guard. It was unusual, sinister, and humiliating. "We were in their sight as grasshoppers," came to my mind as our party climbed the hill.

That night it rained and the next morning we had to return to Base Camp. All the hillsides were slippery and wet. After we had slid and descended for about an hour someone behind me called me. I turned to hear better and slipped. Down I came on a jagged stump—a nasty jolting blow *in the same place as the first blow*. But as I fell, a picture of those young men guarding their demon had flashed before me. I had not been thinking of them, for it took all my wits to keep upright on that slippery slope.

Once down the hill and into civilization I again sought medical advice. An X-ray showed nothing. I felt as if the Lord said, "The time hasn't come yet; get on with your work." And so I did. I was not haunted by any fear of the disease—I had put it deliberately out of my mind and was joyful in my work.

Over a year passed, and physically I had never

felt better in my life. But one day, noticing something not normal in the area where I had twice been hit, I felt I should see Dr. Buker. He looked very serious and said a biopsy should be taken immediately. To my surprise the first report came back, *nonmalignant*. Naturally, John was jubilant, but personally I did not believe it was correct. It is most important, however, never to *act* on these illuminated hunches. I distinguish between the clear voice of God and mere premonitions. I do not hesitate to bank everything on the direct command of the Lord, but I would not act on a mere impression—because, simply, many of my impressions have proved to be false—mere imagination. Satan can distressingly entangle people who acted on their premonitions.

I believe there are some human beings who are psychic. That is, they have powers like clairvoyance and mental telepathy, some more, some less. The Devil plays heyday with this power, of course, and tries to turn the person into a medium for spiritism. But the Holy Spirit can also use this quality to comfort or encourage the Christian who is psychic. It then takes the form of a premonition or *an illuminated hunch*. Now Satan is always ready to pounce on this and turn it to his own advantage. He will stir up spiritual pride over it; and most certainly will try to get the psychic Christian to act on it *before it is proved* whether the claivoyance is correct or imaginary. The only safe way to use such power is to distrust it until its source is manifest. When it is clear that it is given of God then we may humbly extract from it all the comfort we need.

By now I was beginning to believe it was the Lord, not imagination, who had told me nearly two years before that I would develop cancer. But I did not let it occupy my thoughts. I merely wrote two very dear friends about the nonmalignant report. I said, "Pray that if it is wrong I may be alerted in time, and that meanwhile I may be enabled to forget it and get on with my work." That prayer was answered perfectly. Our annual Field Conference was coming very close, and I threw my energies into preparing for it. We house-cleaned every room, and all arrangements were clearly mapped out even to the menu for each day, when Dr. Richard Buker appeared and informed me that a further test of the biopsy was not so optimistic and they felt I should have an operation immediately.

As it happened, a very skillful surgeon was taking a holiday in Chiengmai just those two days and had consented to operate, if I would have it the very next morning. Immediately it was as if the Lord placed a hand on my shoulder and said, *"This is it."*

I had supper guests that night so there was not much time for the flesh to brood over it and get alarmed—which was a kindness.

Just before we left for the hospital the next morning, I turned to see what verse was on my "Choice Gleanings Calendar." It was Psalm 127:2: "For so he giveth his beloved sleep." I was startled. My hunch had spoken of going to America but there had been nothing of *death* in it. Did the Lord—? But I cast it out of my mind as they honked for me to get into the jeep. Just a chance calender verse, anyway. Or was the Lord trying to prepare me? Better not think about it now, on the way to the operation. If it was of the Lord, He would tell me again. So I went cheerfully to the ordeal.

It was most skillfully done and I had every care. Miss Dorothy Jones, R.N., of our Mission "specialed" me and ministered most lovingly. One morning a house doctor came and stood at the foot of my bed and said, "In all my experience I've seen very few patients come through an operation like yours with so little suffering."

"Don't you think it is because I am relaxed, doctor?" I said.

"Undoubtedly. And I used you as an illustration for my class this morning. I told them that they should try to get their patients to put their faith in something outside them—Buddha for the Buddhists, Christ for the Christian—because it would bring relaxation and help them so much." Then he left.

But I lay there thinking. Good psychology, certainly—he is a clever doctor. But how perfectly impossible for a person in such a weak condition to hook his faith onto some nebulae outside himself just because it would be to his benefit if he could! That was not what I was doing! I was resting back on a private word, spoken to me two years before.

Amy Carmichael says this: "Before we reach the place where such waters must be crossed, there is almost always a private word spoken by the Beloved to the lover. That is the word which will be most assaulted as we stand within sight and sound of that seething, roaring flood. The enemy will fasten upon it, twist it about, belittle it, obscure it, try to undermine our confidence in its integrity, and to wreck our tranquillity by making us afraid, but this will put him to flight: *'I believe God that it shall be even as it was told me.'* "

God had told Paul (Acts 23:11): "Be of good

cheer, Paul: for as thou hast testified of me in Jerusalem, so must thou bear witness also at Rome."
This was Paul's *private word;* and when the terrible
storm struck their ship, neither sun nor stars appeared in many days, and all hope that they could
be saved was taken away, Paul stood on that private
word. They would not perish, for God said he was
to see Rome, and, he said quietly, "I believe God."
Paul was not hooking his faith onto some nebulae
outside himself, but onto the word of One whom
he had proved for many years. Even as Paul said, "I
must see Rome," so I relaxed and lay back on the
word, "This is to take me to America." But I must
not yet tell anyone that. The China Inland Mission
does not fly a missionary home to the United States
just because she has had a serious operation. It
would have to be for some special reason, and that
only God should manipulate—I must keep my hands
off. But I quite believed it would happen. Now
nobody had as yet told me that the operation revealed malignancy; when I asked Dr. Buker he
just teased me and avoided a straight answer.

But after I had been home from the hospital about
a week, a letter was handed to us. It contained the
medical report which said it was a fast growing
malignancy and the ordinary estimate would give
me only a year or so to live. But it also advised
my flying to America immediately. The surgeon had
thought he saw traces of it entering the chest, and
the only place in the world where lung cancer could
be cured was in the United States. This advice was
being passed on to Mission Headquarters, and that
is how God manipulated events until His private
word to me had been fulfilled.

Now I had to face the little calendar verse of

the operation morning. Had it been a mere coincidence after all? Or had it been a tender preparation? Time alone will tell.

At first I was startled—I had not expected this. And it was difficult to believe! A month after the operation (which surgeons in America highly praised) I felt normal again. The specialist who examined me was inclined to be quizzical about the melancholy prognostication—he said he found no trace of malignancy left. And so I went about my work, giving it my full attention. But I was, at the same time, making discoveries. I had a new lesson set me, and it is best expressed in the words of II Corinthians 10:5: ". . . casting down imaginations . . . and bringing into captivity every thought to the obedience of Christ."

I found that imagination could give me a bad time. If I coughed, for instance, I immediately had lung cancer (although X-rays showed the chest to be clear)! If I had a toothache, then I was getting cancer of the mouth! And so on. Every tickle or twinge was instantly interpreted as related to my grim enemy. But if I asserted my right to *a sound mind* (II Tim. 1:7), these fears left me and the twinge never developed into anything further. "For God hath not given us the spirit of fear, but of power and of love and of a sound mind." A sound mind is our gift from God, this verse says, but we need to claim it. The American Standard Version translates that word as *discipline*. And the one includes the other, for a sound mind is necessarily a disciplined one.

Thus I was set a new lesson, or an old lesson in a new form. I had to refuse to allow my imagination to play with my future. That future, I believe, is ordered of God, and no man can guess it. For me to let myself imagine how or when the end would come was not only unprofitable, it was definitely harmful, so I had to bring my thoughts into captivity that they might not dishonor the Christ.

The best way to do this, I found, was to engage in some interesting work. While still confined to bed I tried prayer and reading. As I became stronger I set about writing a book—I drew up a daily schedule that would come within the limits of what strength I had, and tried to keep it faithfully. This I enjoyed and can say truthfully that on this platform of a dread disease there have been many months of very real happiness. It makes for health to have a goal and keep on striving for it. Of course I realize that the Lord has been especially good to me in giving me work which is so congenial and yet does not require much physical labor. But I am sure He would have different ideas and helps for others of His children who are on this same platform.

Another thing which has helped me to keep a sound mind is the gathering of the edelweiss of God. I owe this thought to Miss Carmichael. In her book *Gold by Moonlight*, she has a whole chapter on it. Edelweiss grows on barren mountain heights, and its soft beauty is a cheery surprise to the toiling climber. So Miss Carmichael likens it to the little things of joy which can always be found in any painful experience, if only we will gather them as we go along. Sound health and a normal life I cannot have while on this platform; therefore I accept the fact and do not fret about it. But this very trial has brought me unexpected joys and these I dwell on and delight in them as His kind tokens of remembrance. Letters and cards from all over the world have come to me; people I did not know existed are praying for me and they do kind things for me. Is that not delightful? That has enriched my life.

Loving friends have made it possible for us to have our own home—a little apartment, and I have already had our dear son with me longer than a normal furlough would have given. I rejoice in that. Why not? The future of my loved ones, after I leave them? The Lord who has been so kind to me will not be less so to them.

> For my beloved I will not fear: Love knows to do
> For him, for her, from year to year, as hitherto;
> Whom my heart cherishes are dear
> To Thy heart too.
>
> —A. C.

It may not be long before He comes for all His own—then what a foolish waste fretting about it would have been!

My bedroom is kept beautiful with lovely flowers, gifts from loving friends and relatives. That is edelweiss.

Good books are given or lent to me—edelweiss again. Dainty things to eat are brought to our door, but to enumerate all the edelweiss is hopeless. Suffice it to say, much has been given.

What of the dark valley that will inevitably come? I am told that before he died Dr. Harry Rimmer wrote to Dr. Charles Fuller something like this:

> Next Sunday you are to talk about Heaven. I am interested in that land, because I have held a clear title to a bit of property there for over fifty-five years. I did not buy it. It was given to me without money and without price. But the Donor pur-

chased it for me at tremendous sacrifice. I am not holding it for speculation since the title is not transferable. It is not a vacant lot. For more than half a century I have been sending materials out of which the greatest Architect and Builder of the universe has been building a home for me, which will never need to be remodeled or repaired because it will suit me perfectly, individually, and will never grow old. Termites cannot undermine its foundations, for they rest upon the Rock of Ages. Fire cannot destroy it. Floods cannot wash it away. No locks or bolts will ever be placed upon its doors, for no vicious persons can even enter that land where my dwelling stands, now almost completed and almost ready for me to enter in and abide in peace eternally, without fear of being ejected.

There is a valley of deep shadows between the place where I live in California and that to which I shall journey in a very short time. I cannot reach my home in that city of gold without passing through this dark valley of shadows. But I am not afraid, because the best Friend I ever had went through the same valley, long, long ago and drove away all its gloom. He has stuck by me through thick and thin since we first became acquainted fifty-five years ago, and I hold His promise in printed form never to forsake me nor to leave me alone. He will be with me as I walk through the valley of shadows, and I shall not lose my way when He is with me.

Dr. Rimmer has long since arrived in that City of Gold, and I do not know how long was his passage through the valley of shadows. But I have learned this, from my present platform, that the spiritual is tied down to the physical more than is apparent. After my first operation, finding I would have long hours just lying in bed, I said to myself, "Good.

Now I will employ this time in intercession and prayer." But to my surprise and alarm I found I could not! What was wrong with me? Was I backsliding? Then I realized it. To pray for others as I was accustomed to do required *physical* as well as spiritual strength. When I went to gather myself together for this concentrated work, I found there was nothing to gather! Nothing responded to my call. I had no physical strength with which to rally my forces. I just had to lie there and say, "Well, Lord, I will have to ask You to read my heart as You read the names on the breastplate of the high priest in days of yore."

In the same way the exercise of faith requires a physical strength that is not apparent to the well person, nor to the sick person himself if he has never had the experience of physical weakness and sinking. This explains to me myself, at least, why some of the saints have seemed to find the valley of the shadows a dark place. The Lord is most certainly there with them, but the unconscious habitual use of physical strength in laying hold of this fact by faith may disconcert by its absence. To me it is not fair to judge such a person's salvation by what is seen at his deathbed. We do not take seriously what is said in the mutterings of delirium, when a person is not himself. In the same way a Christian's apprehension of Christ should be judged by his lifelong experience of Him, not by what onlookers see during the last hours when the spirit is so hampered by a weakened and dissolving physique. Friends should take comfort in the fact that Christ is there, and the dear one will be consciously in His arms the moment the spirit is free.

I have been reading the diary of David Brainerd

and have noticed the relation between ...ysical well-being or illness and his *sense* ...resence. They were often related. When ...in...body he bemoaned his spiritual barrenness. *"November 1. Was very much disordered in body and sometimes full of pain. . . . Alas! When God is withdrawn, all is gone."* Then a few days later after he was rested a bit, he writes: *"Saw more of the glory and majesty of God . . . than ever I had seen before. . . . Oh, how my soul then rejoiced in God!"* The spirit is not absolutely dependent on physical well-being, as I have myself proved in these pages, but it is more closely related than we are sometimes apt to allow.

Facing the end of one's earthly pilgrimage is not a melancholy thing for a Christian. It is like preparation for the most exciting journey of all. Someone sent me a tract on this subject which I give herewith. It is called "Getting Ready to Move."

The owner of the tenement which I have occupied for many years has given notice that he will furnish but little or nothing for repairs. I am advised to be ready to move.

At first this was not a very welcome notice. The surroundings here are in many respects very pleasant, and were it not for the evidence of decay, I should consider the old house good enough. But even a light wind causes it to tremble and totter and all the braces are not sufficient to make it secure. So I am getting ready to move.

It is strange how quickly one's interest is transferred to the prospective home. I have been consulting maps of the new country and reading descriptions of its inhabitants. One (II Cor. 12:2) who visited it has returned, and from him I learn that it is beautiful beyond description—language breaks down in attempting to tell of what he heard while there. He says that, in order to make an investment there, he has suffered the loss of all things that he owned here, and even rejoices in what others would call making a sacrifice.

Another (John 15:12) whose love to me has been proved by the greatest possible test is now there. He has sent me several clusters of the most delicious fruits. After tasting them, all food here seems insipid.

Two or three times I have been down by the border of the river that forms the boundary, and have wished myself among the company of those who were singing praises to the King on the other side.

Many of my friends have moved there. Before leaving they spoke of my coming later. I have seen the smile upon their faces as they passed out of sight.

Often I am asked to make some new investments here, but my answer in every case, is *"I am getting ready to move."*

This spirit of expectation is our dear inheritance and right. For the Christian, death is not the dissolution of life but the *consummation*.

> The last of life
> For which the first was made,

as Browning puts it.

Or as Amy Carmichael words it, "The days of our bloom and our power are just about to begin."

> Gone, they tell me, is youth;
> Gone is the strength of my life.
> Nothing remains but decline,
> Nothing but age and decay.

Not so, I'm God's little child,
Only beginning to live.
Coming the days of my prime,
Coming the strength of my life,
Coming the vision of God,
Coming my bloom and my power!

Coming the vision of God. Christians often say that the most wonderful thing of all will be to see our Lord face to face. I have pondered that much and feel it is surely worded inadequately. To see the Lord is but a lesser thing to one who has had a close spirit-with-Spirit communion with Him all along. What matter the color of His eyes or the shape of His face? That is not what makes Him precious. Nothing is so deeply intimate as spirit knit with Spirit, and that we can and should enjoy right now while here on earth. I think what is meant is to be with the Lord *with the root of sin gone.* To fellowship with Him without the lazy flesh dragging us back, or unwanted thoughts of pride and self constantly staining us. To be finally rid of corruption, to worship and enjoy Him with heart purged into His own purity, *that* will be an advance over anything that is possible on earth.

And so *the platform of a dread disease becomes but a springboard for Heaven.* We are conformed unto His death. In the pain which is inevitably connected with the descent into the valley of shadows there will be a fellowship, even if not perceived by weakened nature. The power of His resurrection will become known as never before. And the great end, *that I may know Him,* will be granted. We shall be clasped in His arms, we shall rest on His bosom with the impurities of our earth-clogged life gone forever.

It is not death to fling aside this sinful dust,
And rise on strong exulting wing to live among the just.
—C. M.

> They are not lost who find
> The sunset gate, the goal
> Of all their faithful years.
> Not lost are they who reach
> The summit of their climb,
> The peak above the clouds
> And storms. They are not lost
> Who find the light of sun
> And stars and God.
> —H. R. ORR

Oh, fathomless mercy; oh, infinite grace!
With humble thanksgiving the road we retrace;
Thou never hast failed us, our Strength and our Stay;
To whom should we turn for *the rest of the way?*

Through dangers, through darkness, by day
    and by night
Thou ever hast guided, and guided us right.
In Thee we have trusted, and peacefully lay
Our hand in Thy Hand, *for the rest of the way.*
—A. J. FLINT

> Yea, thro' life, death, thro' sorrow and thro' sinning
> He shall suffice me, for He hath sufficed;
> Christ is the end, for Christ was the beginning;
> Christ the beginning, for the end is Christ.
> —F. W. H. M.

Christ? I am Christ's! And let the name suffice you,
Aye, for me, too, He greatly hath sufficed.